James Walker

The altar at home : 2nd series

Selections and prayers for domestic worship

James Walker

The altar at home : 2nd series
Selections and prayers for domestic worship

ISBN/EAN: 9783337283964

Printed in Europe, USA, Canada, Australia, Japan

Cover: Foto ©Andreas Hilbeck / pixelio.de

More available books at **www.hansebooks.com**

THE

ALTAR AT HOME.

SECOND SERIES.

SELECTIONS AND PRAYERS

FOR

DOMESTIC WORSHIP.

. . . . Blest
The home where God is felt.
HEMANS.

FIFTH EDITION

BOSTON:
AMERICAN UNITARIAN ASSOCIATION.
1869.

INTRODUCTION.

IT can hardly be necessary, in view of the constant demand for books of this class, to demonstrate their utility and desirableness, or to apologize for adding one more to the number.

The marked favor with which the *First Series* of the "ALTAR AT HOME" has been received has induced the Editor of the present volume to adopt the general plan of that work.

Many, who have regularly used the "Altar" since its publication, have expressed a wish for a new series of Selections and Prayers, those in the former series, necessarily limited in number, having become somewhat trite from frequent repetition.

While in the present volume the general plan and arrangement of the former issue have been preserved, experience has suggested a few alterations, which it is believed will be generally esteemed as improvements.

The introductory *Selections*, designed to be read in

alternation by the members of the family, have been somewhat extended, while the *Prayers* are generally shorter.

The *Selections* have been made, not exclusively from the Scriptures, but there have been interwoven some of the wise, devout, and elevating thoughts of a few of the purest and most holy men whose existence has blessed the world.

The aim has been to make these *Selections* of a practical character; not simply pious ejaculations, or passages expressive of admitted truths, but those calculated to awaken attention, to produce conviction, to stimulate, to console, to strengthen.

They have been carefully chosen, and so arranged as to follow one another naturally, and be in some sense responsive to each other.

The *verse* of Sacred Poetry which introduces each service, and is designed to be read by the head of the family, or sung by the members of the family when practicable, has been selected as embodying the spirit of the Selections following; to strike the key-note, as it were, of the entire service.

The *Prayers* have been written by a number of clergymen, generally well known in this community, whose names, alphabetically arranged, are given on another page, and to whom the Editor desires to acknowledge his great indebtedness for the essential service rendered him in his laborious and delicate task.

The *Prayers* having been contributed with special reference to the respective services of which they form part, it is believed that a unity of spirit throughout each entire service has been thereby secured, which could not have been attained in any other way.

Another alteration will be noticed in the present series. Instead of dividing the *Selections* into morning and evening services, it has been thought best to append a morning and evening *Prayer* to each *Selection.*

Few families, if any, it is believed, use the book for both morning and evening worship, hence, in the former series, one half the *Selections* were unavailable. By the present arrangement, every *Selection*, except the few designated as "Special," may be used by every family, whether they observe domestic worship statedly at the commencement or at the close of the day. And still further, as, in most instances, the omission of a word or two, or some equally slight change, will make it possible to use the morning and evening *Prayers* interchangeably, the scope of the volume is thereby materially enlarged.

As the First Series of the "ALTAR AT HOME" contains ample selections for the use of the closet, together with the ancient Collects of the Church and a number of Litanies, it. has been thought best to exclude those features from the present work, in order to afford more space for the regular Morning and Evening and Special Services; the practical usefulness of the volume depending, it is believed, upon the extent and variety of these Exercises.

With this brief Introduction, the Editor submits the volume to the acceptance of those for whom it has been prepared, with an earnest hope that it may prove helpful to many households.

J. P. W.

JAMAICA PLAIN, May, 1862.

CONTENTS.

SPECIAL SERVICES.

PRAYERS BY

Rev. E. G. Adams, ... *Templeton, Mass.*
Rev. William R. Alger, ... *Boston.*
Rev. Joseph Allen, D. D. . . . . *Northborough, Mass.*
Rev. C. G. Ames, ... *Bloomington, Ill.*
Rev. George W. Briggs, D. D. . . . . . *Salem, Mass.*
Rev. Charles T. Brooks, ... *Newport, R. I.*
Rev. S. G. Bulfinch, ... *Dorchester, Mass.*
Rev. S. W. Bush, ... *Medfield, Mass.*
Rev. J. F. Clarke, ... *Boston.*
Rev. Robert Collyer, ... *Chicago, Ill.*
Rev. Rufus Ellis, ... *Boston.*
Rev. Henry W. Foote, ... *Boston.*
Rev. Edward E. Hale, ... *Boston.*
Rev. F. H. Hedge, D. D. . . . . *Brookline, Mass.*
Rev. Alonzo Hill, D. D. . . . . *Worcester, Mass.*
Rev. Thomas Hill, D. D. . . . . *Yellow Springs, Ohio.*
Rev. George W. Hosmer, D. D. . . . . *Buffalo, N. Y.*
Rev. L. J. Livermore, ... *Lexington, Mass.*
Rev. Charles Lowe, ... *Somerville, Mass.*
Rev. John H. Morison, D. D. . . . . . *Milton, Mass.*
Rev. A. B Muzzey, ... *Newburyport, Mass*
Rev. Samuel Osgood, D. D. . . . . . . *New York.*
Rev. A. P. Peabody, D. D. . . . . *Cambridge.*
Rev. Richard Pike, ... *Dorchester, Mass.*
Rev. E. W. Reynolds, ... *Watertown, N. Y.*
Rev. Chandler Robbins, D. D. . . . . . *Boston.*
Rev. R. R. Shippen, ... *Worcester, Mass.*
Rev. N. A. Staples, ... *Brooklyn, N. Y.*
Rev. Horatio Stebbins, ... *Portland, Me.*
Rev. J. W. Thompson, D. D. . . . . . . *Jamaica Plain, Mass.*
Rev. James Walker, D. D. . . . . . . *Cambridge.*
Rev. Augustus Woodbury, ... *Providence, R. I.*

I and my house are ready, Lord,
With hearts that beat in sweet accord,
To serve thee and obey thee;
Be in the midst of us, we pray,
To guide and bless us, that we may
A willing service pay thee:
Of us all,
Great and small,
Make a pious congregation,
Pure in life and conversation.

Let thy good spirit by the word
Work mightily in us, O Lord,
Our souls and bodies filling!
O let the sun of grace shine bright,
That there may be abundant light
In us and in our dwelling:
On our way,
Night and day,
With the heavenly manna feed us,
To the heavenly Canaan lead us.

Send peace and blessing from above,
Unite us all in faith and love
    Who in this house are living;
Let charity our hearts prepare
To suffer long, and all things bear,
    Meek, gentle, and forgiving;
Nor in aught
Christ hath taught
Let us fail to one another,
But each to love and help his brother.

Lord, let our house be built upon
Thy faithfulness and grace alone;
    And when the day is closing,
And night her gloomy shadow flings,
Let us lie down beneath thy wings
    With childlike trust reposing;
E'en with smart
In the heart,
Cheerful, happy, and confiding,
Patiently in thee abiding.

                   LYRA DOMESTICA.

Altar at Home.

I.

DOMESTIC LOVE AND UNITY.

Help us to help each other, Lord,
Each other's cross to bear ;
Let each his friendly aid afford,
And feel his brother's care.

Help us to build each other up ;
Our little stock improve ;
Increase our faith, confirm our hope,
And perfect us in love.
WESLEY'S COLL.

Be kindly affectioned one to another with brotherly love ; in honor preferring one another.

How good and pleasant it is for brethren to dwell together in unity !

Be ye all of one mind, having compassion one of another ; love as brethren, be pitiful, be courteous :

Not rendering evil for evil, or railing for railing ; but contrariwise blessing.

Learn first to show piety at home, for that is good and acceptable before God.

1

Avoid foolish questions, and contentions and strivings, for they are unprofitable and vain.

Bear ye one another's burdens, and so fulfil the law of Christ.

Ye younger submit yourselves unto the elder. Yea, all of you be subject one to another, and be clothed with humility.

Let us love one another; for love is of God; and every one that loveth is born of God, and knoweth God.

But he that hateth his brother is in darkness, and walketh in darkness, and knoweth not whither he goeth.

May God grant, that, as we are all members of the same body, have one and the same Father, the same Saviour, we may live in unity and godly love, and be charitable according to our ability.

Let it please thee to bless the house of thy servant, that it may be before thee forever; for thou blessest, O Lord, and it shall be blessed forever.

MORNING.

O THOU, in whom all the families of the earth are blessed, we thank thee that we are again permitted to offer our united praise and supplication at the household altar. We bless thee for the assurance, that, where two or three are met together in the Saviour's name, they have his presence, sympathy, and love. We remember with gratitude the kind Providence that has been over us through the whole of our united life, making our home happy, and enabling us to minister in so many ways to one another's well-being. Help us to live together, as the dying ought to live with reference to the things that change and perish, as the undying ought to live in the view of things unseen and eternal. May we watch for one another's religious good, spiritual peace, and enduring joy. May we bear one another's burdens, and help one another's infirmities. May we move on together in every way of duty, looking unto Jesus, and seeking to plant our footsteps where he has trodden. May we be united in the love of God, the faith of Christ, the pursuit of all that is pure and true, noble and heavenly. May we so dwell together, while our house is of clay and our habitation in the dust, that we may dwell together in the house not made with hands.

We pray for all whom thou hast made ours, that thou wouldst guide them by thy counsel, and cheer them by the assurance of thy redeeming love. And while we commend to thee those who are still around us, we would recognize our unbroken union with those faithful and beloved friends who have passed away from our sight, and have entered before us into thy rest. May their felt sympathy be with us in duty and in trial, strengthening and gladdening us continually, and giving us an ever more intimate home-feeling for the mansions in the Father's house on high. Command thy blessing on all men every-

where, and may the light of thy love shine in all
lands and into all hearts.

Our Father, hear our prayer, and forgive and
accept us, now and evermore, through thy mercy in
Jesus Christ our Saviour. *Amen.*

EVENING.

UNIVERSAL Sovereign, Father of all spirits,
as the shades of night gather around our
dwelling, we kneel together at the domestic altar
and beseech thee to guard and bless us. O may
no shades of evil fall on us, no suspicions or alterations alienate our now united hearts.

Thou art pleased to see thy children live together in love. May our love be so pure and fervent as to form an acceptable part of the worship
we render to thee. We would bear each other in
affectionate remembrance amidst all the round of
daily toil and temptation, each striving to be worthy of the other, and all to be found faithful before
thee. In our mutual relations we would be forbearing, patient, generous, devoted to each other's
good, in the kind correction of faults and cordial
co-operation in the culture of excellence. We supplicate grace to appropriate to their divinest uses
all thine appointments, whether of prosperity or
adversity. Guard our fold from ravage. Deliver
us from an ungrateful and rebellious spirit. What-

ever thou doest, may we be resigned to thy will, confident that the end will compensate and justify all.

In the beloved name of Christ may we say, Thy will be done. *Amen.*

II.

AGAINST WORLDLY-MINDEDNESS.

Without Thy presence, wealth is bags of cares;
Wisdom but folly; joy, disquiet, sadness;
Friendship is treason, and delights are snares;
Pleasures but pain, and mirth but pleasing madness.
FRANCIS QUARLES.

He that loveth life for the sake of the pleasures and advantages it affords, will soon lose the love of heavenly things; the love of God, of his soul, and of the duty he owes to them. — *Wilson.*

What shall it profit a man, if he shall gain the whole world, and lose his own soul?

How many perish by reason of vain learning in this world, who take little care of the serving of God. — *A Kempis.*

He that received seed among the thorns is he that heareth the word; and the care of this world, and the deceitfulness of riches, choke the word, and he becometh unfruitful.

Let me not be overcome, O Lord, let me not be overcome

by flesh and blood; let not the world and the brief glory thereof deceive me. — *À Kempis.*

Thou sayest, I am rich, increased with goods, and have need of nothing; and knowest not that thou art wretched, and miserable, and poor, and blind, and naked.

Shut my heart, O Lord, against the love of worldly riches, lest I betray thee as Judas did. — *Wilson.*

Turn away mine eyes from beholding vanity; and quicken thou me in thy way.

Let your conversation be without covetousness; and be content with such things as ye have; for he hath said, I will never leave thee nor forsake thee.

The world passeth away, and the lust thereof; but he that doeth the will of God abideth forever.

MORNING.

THE earth is thine, O God, and its fulness is thy blessed gift. May we accept all things from thee and love and enjoy thee in all things. Yet, All-Holy One, we do humbly confess that these worldly goods, which are thy creatures, do too often estrange us from thee, the Creator, and that they tempt us too much to self-indulgence and pride and vanity. Forgive us this one too-ready sin, and help us to watch more jealously, and guard more resolutely, against this ever-present temptation.

May we regard every good gift as the reason of a deeper responsibility, instead of a lure to pleasure or a spur to self-conceit. Sacredly may we hold

all our talents as under stewardship from God, and
may the weight of them bow us down more humbly
before thy mercy-seat. May we care more to be-
friend the lowly than to flatter and to feast the
rich and powerful, and may we so employ our time
and means as to lay up the goods that will remain
with us when earthly friends and favors vanish.

All-Wise and All-Holy, graciously animate us
with a true purpose, a pervading and unwavering
determination to do all our work as within thy
kingdom, and hold our business, our home, and
our pleasures in subjection to thy laws. Help us
to bear reverses so patiently and humbly as to save
us alike from envy of our neighbor's prosperity and
from repining at thy good Providence. Enable us
to consecrate duly our joys, that when we are happy
our blessedness may be in thee, our God, and so our
joys shall rise and make our children and friends
rise in faith and gratitude toward thee.

In thy mercy forgive our overweening love of the
world, and establish us in the fellowship that is
divine and abiding, through him who for us overcame the world, even Jesus Christ our Lord.
Amen.

EVENING.

O GOD, our Heavenly Father, grant, we beseech thee, that a sense of thy nearness and

thy holiness may draw us away from every inordinate attachment to the transitory, unsatisfying
things of time. Save us from worldliness and sin.
Guard us against the insidious and deceitful arts
which would blind us to our highest good and bring
us into subjection to the world. Teach us to have
our conversation in heaven. Let us not wander
away from our heavenly home, but, while our hands
and thoughts are engaged amid the cares and employments of time, grant that we may bring with us
into these employments the spirit of thine heavenly
kingdom, and be inspired and guided by it wherever
we go. Thou, who embracest all beings and all
worlds as if they were one, and who carest for
every one of us as if he were the whole universe,
enfold us in thy love, breathe into us thy gentle and
holy spirit, and so win us to thyself, that neither
the world nor the things of the world shall gain
dominion over us, or estrange us from Him who
alone can satisfy the heart, in whose presence is
fulness of joy, and at whose right hand are pleasures for evermore, through Jesus Christ our Lord.
Amen.

III.

THE GOODNESS OF GOD.

The Lord is never far away,
*   Nor sundered from his flock ;*
He is their refuge and their stay,
*   Their peace, their trust, their rock,*
And with a mother's watchful love
He guides them wheresoe'er they rove.
J. J. SCHUTZ.

O give thanks unto the Lord, for he is good ; for his mercy endureth forever.

Blessed be the Lord, who daily loadeth us with benefits, even the God of our salvation.

For the Lord is good; his mercy is everlasting; and his truth endureth to all generations.

The Lord is merciful and gracious, slow to anger, and plenteous in mercy.

Like as a father pitieth his children, so the Lord pitieth them that fear him.

Thou, Lord, art good, and ready to forgive ; and plenteous in mercy unto all them that call upon thee.

O give thanks unto the Lord; call upon his name: make known his deeds among his people.

God is great, therefore will he be sought; he is good, therefore will he be found. — *J. Mason.*

Seek the Lord, and his strength; seek his face evermore.

He is the Lord our God; his judgments are in all the earth.

This is the covenant that I will make with the house of Israel, saith the Lord: I will put my laws into their mind, and write them in their hearts: and I will be to them a God, and they shall be to me a people.

For I will be merciful to their unrighteousness, and their sins and their iniquities will I remember no more.

Having these promises, let us cleanse ourselves from all filthiness of the flesh and spirit, perfecting holiness in the fear of the Lord.

MORNING.

WE would render thanks unto thee, O Lord, for thou art good, and thy mercy endureth forever. We would praise thee for thy goodness, and for thy wonderful works to the children of men. And may we learn, with devout thankfulness, to connect the thought of thy goodness with every event of life and every gift of thy love, till thou hast become to us, as thou art, the all-embracing influence in which we live, — the fountain of every pure affection, — the author of every dear and holy inspiration, — the atmosphere of love in which we may bathe our souls with an infinite joy, — not afar off, but a present helper in every time of need, ready to hear and answer wherever there is a heart yearning for thee, — thou bestower of all that crowns our happiness on earth, or that turns our sorrows into blessings, — who art always waiting to be gracious, to renew our minds with ever-enlarging and uplifting thoughts, to refresh our hearts with affections ever more expansive and devout. We thank thee for what our eyes are permitted to see, for this world of order and beauty which lies around us ; but more heartily we thank thee for what our eyes cannot see, — for the holy, loving Providence which hems us in by defences too delicate and gentle to be perceived, — for the hidden, but divine benignity which rules the tempest, scatters the hoar-frost like ashes, imprisons the arctic seas in ice, breathes upon us in the morning light and summer breeze, enfolds us in darkness and sleep, guides the sun and stars in their course, and, in all times of prosperity or tribulation, waits with love and tenderness on every defenceless and humble soul.

May we feel that, while we live in thee, no evil can approach to do us harm, and that amid the fiercest violence of the tempest, or of disease, the little child, wrapt in its own sweet and trusting innocence, is surrounded and protected by a power mightier than all the outward storm and strife. We thank thee, O God, for the assurance of thy love in Jesus Christ, for the grace, mercy, and truth which have flowed into the world through him, and in which we may rejoice with joy unspeakable, and full of glory. May we be made partakers of these, the richest of thy gifts, and through him, in thy holy spirit, ascribe unto thee honor and praise, for ever and ever. *Amen.*

EVENING.

OUR Heavenly Father, thou whose goodness is beyond the power of human language to express, we thank thee for thy daily care and providence. May our minds be filled with the recollection of thy mercies. Every day is rich with the tokens of thy love. Thou openest thy hand, and we are filled with good. Grant that, while the recipients of thy constant kindness, we may accept thy gifts with grateful affection and faithful obedience. As we recall thy manifold bounties, we would especially thank thee for the revelation of thyself which thou hast made through thy beloved Son, Jesus Christ. We rejoice that he has taught us to call thee Our Father. With grateful trust may we feel that, in this hour of our evening devotions, while we are kneeling at the family altar. thou art nearer to us than our dearest earthly friend; that the tie which binds our hearts to thee is more enduring than those which bind us as a family by the sweet and tender relations of domestic life. Thou lovest each of thy children with a deeper and more constant love than that which a mother has for her child. Though we are weak and sinful, though we receive thy free gifts with murmurs and dissatisfaction, though we complain at our lot, and sometimes even question thy moral government, still thou dost bear with our ingratitude, and art ever desirous to bless and sanctify each of thy children. Thy love never fails. Thou makest the sun to rise on the evil and the good, and sendest rain on the just and the unjust. Grant, as thus we remember thy universal and impartial goodness, we may learn to trust thine unfailing compassion. If burdened with the conviction of sin, may we learn to rely on thy pity. In grief thou art our comforter, in trial our refuge, in trouble our peace, in sorrow our stay and joy. With penitent hearts we would seek thy forgiveness. Grant us the smile of thy countenance and the peace of reconciliation. May we rely upon thy Providence, and learn to bear our trials in patience, bravely striving against temptation; accepting the afflictions of our lot with cheerful submission, and the undoubting faith that thou wilt lead us through darkness, struggle, and anguish to purity, peace, and joy, and that thus we may reap the fruits of a Christian experience, and grow daily in the knowledge of the wisdom and love of thee, and a more unfailing obedience to the precepts of thy Son, Jesus Christ. And unto thee, the King immortal, eternal, the only true God, be glory forever. *Amen.*

I V.

PERSONAL PIETY.

Still to the lowly soul
He doth Himself impart,
And for His cradle and His throne
Chooseth the pure in heart.

KEBLE.

In the morning fix thy good purpose; and at night examine thyself what thou hast done, how thou hast behaved thyself in word, deed, and thought. — *À Kempis.*

Add to your faith, virtue; and to virtue, knowledge; and to knowledge, temperance; and to temperance, patience; and to patience, godliness;

And to godliness, brotherly kindness; and to brotherly kindness, charity.

For if these things be in you, and abound, they make you that ye shall neither be barren nor unfruitful in the knowledge of our Lord Jesus Christ.

Piety, which is a true devotion to God, consists in doing all his will precisely at the time, in the situation, and under the circumstances, in which he has placed us. — *Fénelon.*

Piety supplieth us with business of a most worthy nature, and lofty importance; it engageth us to free our minds from all fond conceits and cleanse our hearts from all corrupt affections;

To curb our brutish appetites, to tame our wild passions, to correct our perverse inclinations, to conform the dispositions of our soul, and the actions of our life, to the eternal laws of righteousness and goodness. — *Dr. Barrow.*

Thou wilt never be thus inwardly religious, unless thou pass over other men's matters with silence, and look especially to thyself. — *À Kempis.*

No man can hinder our private addresses to God, every man can build a chapel in his breast, himself the priest, his heart the sacrifice, and the earth he treads on the altar. — *Taylor.*

MORNING.

O THOU who hast scattered the shades of night by the bright beams of the dawn, and in thy tender mercy hast safely brought us to the beginning of this new day; shine into our hearts, we beseech thee, with the light of thy truth; dispel all dark thoughts from our minds, and blot out our sins as the morning cloud.

Precious, O Lord, are thy gifts, which are new to us every morning and every night: dear to us are the earthly comforts which thou hast kindly provided, — our home, our friends, our daily bread, and our nightly rest; — and for them all and each we offer our humble thanksgivings. But more precious than all to us, O our Heavenly Father, is that faith in thy infinite goodness, and that hope in thy never-failing mercy, with which thou hast inspired our souls through thy beloved Son. For him, thine unspeakable gift, the brightness of thy paternal glory, the true and unfading light of life,

we would bless thee when we lie down and when
we rise up, when morning rises in brightness, or
night gathers in gloom.   Let the sweet and sacred
thought of him dwell in our minds, and his pure
influence abide with us all the day long; to save
us from the power of sin, to win us from the allurements of evil, and to draw us nearer to thee.   May
the Good Shepherd lead us forth to the duties of
this day, as he doth his own flock, going before
us to guide and to guard; and may we meekly
and obediently follow him, listening to his voice as
it calls, and teaches, and warns, and comforts us;
and not hearkening to the voice of strangers, who
have no love nor pity for our souls.   In every
condition and circumstance of life may we look
unto him, to know what is our duty and to obtain
strength to perform it.   May we learn of him how
to maintain a lowly mind, and yet an aspiring spirit;
how to suffer, and yet rejoice ; not to resist evil,
and still to overcome it; to live in the world, and
yet to live above the world.

O gracious Lord, what treasures of wisdom and
love and blessedness hast thou hid for us, thy frail
and erring, and yet most favored children, in thy
Son !   Let them be the chosen object of our study
and pursuit, before all riches, and learning, and
earthly honors and rewards.

May the eyes of our understanding be enlightened, that we may know what is the hope of his

calling, and what are the riches of the glory of his inheritance in the saints, and what is the exceeding greatness of his power to bless and to save all those who believe in him. May we be able to comprehend, with all his true disciples, what is the breadth and length and depth and height; and to know the love of Christ, which passeth knowledge, that we may be filled with all the fulness of God.

Now unto Him who is able to do for us exceeding abundantly, above all that we can ask or think, be glory and honor, through Jesus Christ, for ever and ever. *Amen.*

EVENING.

O GOD, thou who art the source of every blessing, the giver of every good and perfect gift, grant us the aid of thy Holy Spirit, that we may be sanctified, and made the recipients of rich love and indwelling peace. We need thy forgiveness, and would seek thy favor. Trusting in thy free and boundless grace, we most earnestly desire that thou wouldst take up thy abode in our hearts. Make us wholly thine. Without thee we are nothing, and can do nothing. But in our weakness and poverty of soul thou hast promised to hear our cry. Keep us from sin. We need thee. We seek thee. Come now, O God, in thine infinite mercy, and bless us, thine offending children. Spare us, good

Lord. Stir our souls to greater diligence, and quicken within us more devout aspiration. May our consciences be pierced with the arrow of contrition, so that, through the conviction of past sins and the spiritual renewal of faith, we may be born anew in Christ Jesus. By the constant renewing of our minds, may we walk with him in the regeneration, and grow daily into the knowledge and love of thee, and obedience to thy commandments. We pray for the members of this household, and and may each give to thee the heart's sincere and lowly service. Grant that there may be in each of our souls a true Bethel, from which shall arise the lowly incense of pure devotion, and may the offering thus holy and acceptable in thy sight bring to thy children the angel ministries of purity and peace.

We plead with thee for a more sanctified life. Lift us up out of sin and folly. May we feel thy presence, and see thy smile, and through a personal experience taste of the richness and know the joys of true piety. Thou wilt dwell near thy lowly children : may we welcome thee to our hearts, so that we may know the height and depth, the length and breadth, of the love of thee. May we daily grow into a knowledge of thy goodness, live more devoted to thy service, and more singly to thy glory. And thine shall be the praise, through Christ our Redeemer. *Amen.*

V.

ACTIVE VIRTUE.

Action still must wait on thought ;
Life 's a voyage, rough though short ;
We must dare the sorrow-wave,
Many a sin-storm we must brave,
Ere we reach our destined port.

ANON.

Let your light so shine before men, that they may see your good works, and glorify your Father which is in heaven.

A contemplative life, which does not cast any beam of heat or light upon human society, is not known to divinity. — *Bacon.*

Let us do good unto all men.

For not the hearers of the law are just before God, but the doers of the law shall be justified.

Men should know that, in this theatre of man's life, it is reserved only for God and angels to be lookers-on. — *Bacon.*

Seeing that the love of God is never standing idle, so be ye constantly abounding in good works, enduring all that befalls you cheerfully, for God's sake. — *Tauler.*

The works of mercy are so many as the affections of mercy have objects, or as the world hath kinds of misery. — *Taylor.*

God is the fountain of honor ; and the conduit by which he conveys it to the sons of men are virtues and generous practices. — *South.*

The grand deciding question at the last day will be, not,

What have you said? or, What have you believed? but, What have you done more than others? — *South.*

Be ye doers of the word, not hearers only.

Then shall the king say, Come, ye blessed of my Father, inherit the kingdom prepared for you from the foundation of the world.

For I was an hungered, and ye gave me meat; I was thirsty, and ye gave me drink; I was a stranger, and ye took me in; naked, and ye clothed me; I was sick, and ye visited me; I was in prison, and ye came unto me.

MORNING.

MERCIFUL God, whose loving-kindness never slumbers nor sleeps, we thank thee for the secure repose of the night, and for the returning blessings of the day. To thee and thy service would we surrender all the powers with which thou hast endowed us. In gladness and gratitude would we offer our whole being, as a living sacrifice, on the altar of love and duty. We seek the wisdom which cometh from above to guide us in the employment of our time and in the direction of our labors. May we be inspired with love for thee and for all thou hast made; and permit us to be thy ministers of peace and good-will to men. May it be our meat and drink to do thy will. May we be ready to every good word and work, regardless of our selfish interests, and unmoved by the smiles or frowns of the world.

Father, deliver us from evil! Save us from ourselves. May we be victorious over pride and passion, over self-will and sensuality. Purify our hearts and enlighten our eyes, that we may know the meaning and the uses of life, and that we may see thee in all events and in all thy works. May our existence be sacred to us, because we are thy children, continually having our being in thee. In all our daily duties, may we rejoice that we are workers together with God. So help us to follow Christ by patient continuance in well-doing, till thy grace shall exalt us to share his glory at thy right hand forevermore. *Amen.*

EVENING.

WE bless thee, all-perfect Father, for thy presence, thy strength, and thy comforts granted us during the hours of this day. Without thee, we should have nothing and be nothing. But thou hast been pleased to appoint that thy purposes should be carried forward by the efforts which thy children make according to thy Holy Word. With our human weakness and frailty thine infinite power and providence come into union; and thou hast taught us that we should work for the same great ends for which thou, by thy Spirit, art working. In every effort to do thy will may we feel that we have a true oneness with all who love thy com-

mands, whether on earth or in heaven; and a
oneness with our blessed Master and Saviour, and
through him with thyself. May we not shun
the occasions which offer for doing good by the
sacrifice of our inclinations or convenience. May
we go forward through every conflict where duty
calls, in the strength of the Lord our God. May
it seem to us a small thing to be judged of man's
judgment, but may our own hearts condemn us
not. Fill us with that love and trust which cast
out fear. May our souls be in sympathy with
them who are in adversity, and with all who are
under any manner of wrong or oppression from
evil men. May our words ever be faithful, and
our action earnest and effectual, to relieve sorrow,
and to build up thy kingdom in the world, according to the Gospel of our Lord Jesus Christ.
Amen.

VI.

CONFESSION OF SIN.

Foolish fears and fond desires,
Vain regrets for things as vain;
Lips too seldom taught to praise,
Oft to murmur and complain:
These and every secret fault,
Filled with grief and shame, we own;
Humbled at thy feet we lie,
Seeking pardon at thy throne.

JOHN TAYLOR.

I will confess against myself mine own unrighteousness; I will confess my weakness unto thee, O Lord. — *À Kempis.*

Whoso confesseth and forsaketh his sin shall have mercy.

He that confesses with his tongue, and wants confession in his heart, is either a vain man or a hypocrite:

He that hath confession in his heart, and wants it on his tongue, is either a proud man, or a timorous. — *Bp. Hall.*

I have sinned against Heaven, and in thy sight.

O Lord God, behold, we are before thee in our trespasses; we cannot stand before thee for this.

I acknowledge my sin unto thee, O God, and mine iniquities will I not hide.

I am merciful, saith the Lord, and I will not keep anger forever. Only acknowledge thine iniquity, that thou hast transgressed against the Lord thy God.

If we confess our sins, God is faithful and just to forgive us our sins, and to cleanse us from all unrighteousness.

Examine diligently thy conscience, and to the utmost of thy power purify and make it clear, with true contrition and humble confession ; so as there may be nothing in thee that may weigh heavy upon thee, or may breed in thee remorse of conscience. — *À Kempis.*

He that covereth his sins shall not prosper ; but whoso confesseth and forsaketh them shall have mercy.

We have sinned, and have committed iniquity, and have done wickedly, and have rebelled, even by departing from thy precepts.

To the Lord our God belong mercies and forgivenesses, though we have rebelled against him.

O Lord, hear ! O Lord, forgive ! O Lord, hearken, and do ! defer not.

For I acknowledge my transgressions ; and my sin is ever before me.

Wash me thoroughly from mine iniquity, and cleanse me from my sin.

MORNING.

GOD over all, forever blessed ! the new light of this new day is from thee, and as it shines about us we would come into thy presence, O thou everlasting Father and Friend. Meet us in our coming, we pray thee, and out of thine abounding grace in Christ Jesus minister to our heart's necessities. Thou seest what we are. Our foolishness and our sins are known to thee; and even to us, blind and wayward as we are, they are grievous and reproachful. We would confess them and forsake them. Let them not hinder our coming to thee, but may we have entire faith in that most tender love which looks out upon us through the face of the Lord Jesus, and saith unto us by his lips, " Thy sins are forgiven thee." O thou blessed Spirit of power and goodness! help us this day to keep thy commandments. Enlarge our hearts unto those high measures of fidelity and patience and charity! May we worship and do thy sweet and holy will. Let that which is perfect come within us, and that which is in part shall be done away! Reconcile us unto thyself! May we be born of water and of the spirit! May we be saved henceforth from everything evil and unlovely! Thy grace, O Lord, shall be sufficient for us, and we will strive to lay hold of thy strong and gentle hand, and though our steps should falter for a moment, thou wilt hold us up in thy paths. Make this day a day of love and faithfulness;—love in our hearts and in our household; faithfulness in all that our lips find to utter, in all that our hands find to do. May those who are dear to our hearts be enriched with the frequency of the Holy Spirit, and with the treasures that are laid up in heaven, until we shall all come in the unity of the faith and the knowledge of the Son of God unto a

2

perfect man, unto the measure of the stature of the fulness of Christ, for whom we thank thee and in whom we adore and bless thee. *Amen.*

EVENING.

OUR Father, who art in heaven, hallowed be thy name. At the close of another day of our brief earthly life, through which thy hand has supported and thy love has blessed us, we, thy frail and erring children, would reverently kneel before thy throne, to thank thee for thy unmerited favors and offer our evening prayer.

From this fleeting world, with all its engrossing cares and vanities, from all our wanderings of thought and way, O holy and merciful Father, we would now return to thee, with penitence and filial trust. Receive us, we beseech thee, and look down graciously upon us, though we bring only that sacrifice of a contrite heart, which thy sacred word has assured us thou wilt not despise. We earnestly desire to be at peace with thee. We would be sorry for everything in our lives which has been contrary to thy holy will, and prevented our hearts from communing with and enjoying thee. The experience of another period of action and trial has deepened our sense of imperfection and unworthiness. We have left undone those things which we ought to have done, and we have done those things which we ought not to have done. We have not lived as thy children, nor sought to glorify thee as our Heavenly Father. Our affections have been too strongly set upon earthly things. We have not always enjoyed thy gifts with a lively gratitude, nor borne our disappointments with a cheerful submission. We have not watched against temptation, nor strenuously resisted it. We have not had our conversation in the world in simplicity and godly sincerity; nor diligently practised self-denial, humility, brotherly kindness, and charity. Our own hearts, O God, as we search them before thee, condemn us of doubts and fears, follies and impurities, vain thoughts and unholy desires, unchristian feelings, words, and deeds. Thou art greater than our hearts in knowledge of our sins. And, blessed be thy name, thou art greater also in forgiveness, and in power to purge away our transgressions, and to renew and sanctify us in the spirit of our minds. Have mercy upon us, O Lord, according to thy loving-kindness; for we acknowledge our transgressions. Hide thy face from our sins, and blot out all our iniquities. Create in us a clean heart, O God; and renew a right spirit within us. Cast us not away from thy presence; and take not thy Holy Spirit from us. In the name of thy blessed Son, who came from thy bosom to manifest thy mercy towards our erring race, to invite sinners to repentance, and to seal thy promise of

pardon in his most precious blood, we now supplicate thy forgiveness ; and commending ourselves, in
humble trust, to thy compassion and protecting care,
will lay us down in hope, and sleep. Guard us,
O thou Keeper of Israel, through the hours of
darkness, from all harm and danger, from all dis-
quieting thoughts and evil influences, and wake us,
if it be thy good pleasure, in the morning, refreshed and renewed by sweet and pure slumbers,
to praise thee with new gratitude and serve thee
with new obedience, among the faithful and joyous
believers in Jesus Christ, our Redeemer. *Amen.*

VII.

THE BREVITY OF LIFE.

Teach me the measure of my days,
Thou maker of my frame ;
I would survey life's narrow space,
And learn how frail I am.

WATTS.

Behold, thou hast made my days as a handbreadth ; and
mine age is as nothing before thee : verily, every man at his
best state is altogether vanity.

O how wise and happy is he that now laboreth to be such

an one in his life, as he wisheth to be found at the hour of his death. — *À Kempis.*

One generation passeth away, and another generation cometh ; but the earth abideth forever.

Here we have no continuing city, but we seek one to come.

What man is he that desireth life, and loveth many days, that he may see good ? Keep thy tongue from evil, and thy lips from speaking guile. Depart from evil, and do good; seek peace and pursue it.

What is your life ? It is even a vapor, that appeareth for a little time, and then vanisheth away.

We spend our years as a tale that is told. So teach us to number our days, that we may apply our hearts unto wisdom.

Life is a smile that flutters on our lips, a shadow, an appearance, a dewdrop, a breath, a dream, a torrent which flows away. — *St. Gregory.*

Yet this very instability of human things, O blessed wisdom of God, is in the perfection of thy decrees ; that by it we may be compelled to seek after solid and unchangeable good. — *St. Gregory.*

Happy is the man that findeth wisdom, and the man that getteth understanding.

Length of days is in her right hand ; and in her left hand riches and honor.

The fear of the Lord is the beginning of wisdom ; and the knowledge of the holy is understanding.

Though a sinner do evil an hundred times, and his days be prolonged, yet surely I know that it shall be well with them that fear God. But it shall not be well with the wicked.

MORNING.

ETERNAL God, to whom our mortal years are but a span, — Author and Sustainer of our being, — with a solemn sense of the great mystery of life, we would welcome this new day as a gift from thee. And while we rejoice in the anticipations with which we are permitted to look forward to its hours, we would realize also the uncertainty of all, as we remember how frail we are. Even the bright return of morning reminds us of the rapidity of time and change.

Yet, O thou God of infinite love, we thank thee that this solemn thought is not a thought of gloom, but that, though we are indeed like the grass of the field in our frailty and the insecurity of our days, yet, amid all the uncertainty, there is something sure. Though the grass withereth and the flower fadeth, the word of the Lord abideth forever. To that enduring word, O God, we turn. It gives us a promise of a life that knows no blight nor change. It tells us of heaven, and of thy unfailing love. It speaks to us of Jesus, the Way and Guide to thee. O, may the thought of these blessed realities sanctify the hours of this present day. And while we consider the shortness of our lives, may we be mindful of the preciousness of every passing moment. May we remember that every hour brings its sacred responsibilities, and opens to us its holy uses and ways of attaining eternal good. O grant that we may be faithful to them all. Let it not be that we shall any longer turn a deaf ear to the voice which calls us to glory and immortality. May we so live, with our lamps trimmed and burning, that, whenever the Bridegroom cometh, we shall meet him with joy; and may these days of our earthly life, however few they are, be rich in those imperishable fruits which shall abide with us forever.

Father, hear us in this our prayer, and keep us in thy fear, through thine infinite mercy, revealed to us in Jesus Christ. *Amen.*

EVENING.

ALMIGHTY God, our Heavenly Father; thou who art from everlasting to everlasting; we, thy children, whose days are numbered, and whose years come to an end, bow before thee at this evening hour, in humble acknowledgment of our dependence. We desire to lift up our hearts to thee in grateful homage, that thou hast preserved us through another day and hast been very gracious and merciful to us. We would remember and confess before thee, O God, our imperfections and our sins. We have not had thee in all our thoughts; we have not walked according to thy law and thy commandments in all our ways; we have not been followers together of the Lord Jesus Christ in all that we have done. Do thou forgive us, our Heavenly Father; and blot out our iniquities, and give us grace and strength from heaven henceforth to be thy obedient children.

We would remember before thee, O God, our mortality. So teach us to number our days that we may apply our hearts unto wisdom. Give us grace to realize that we are but sojourners in our earthly homes, and that we must all, sooner or later, follow on after the generations who have gone before us. Help us, O God, we beseech thee, to be faithful and diligent in our appointed sphere of labor and duty during the time allotted to us in this present life, that we may be prepared for the change which awaits us, and ready for our departure at thine own summons. Impress upon our hearts, we beseech thee, a devout sense of the sacredness of the opportunities and privileges which thou art every day granting us, and, as the time is short, teach us how to make a wise use of them in the days or years which remain to us in this world.

O God, at this evening hour we would remember before thee our friends and all who have an interest in our hearts, and commend them to thy fatherly care and blessing, and to the teachings of thy Holy Spirit.

Bless the whole world, we beseech thee, with a knowledge of the truth as it is in Jesus Christ; and may the time speedily come when all nations and all people shall render unto thee the homage of obedience and love. And thine shall be the praise for-evermore. *Amen.*

VIII.

SEEING GOD IN HIS WORKS.

Thou art, O God, the life and light
Of all this wondrous world we see ;
Its glow by day, its smile by night,
Are but reflections caught from thee ;
Where'er we turn, thy glories shine,
And all things fair and bright are thine.

MOORE.

The heavens declare the glory of God ; and the firmament showeth his handiwork.

Day unto day uttereth speech, and night unto night showeth knowledge.

By the word of the Lord were the heavens made ; and all the host of them by the breath of his mouth.

For he spake, and it was done ; he commanded, and it stood fast.

The day is thine, the night also is thine : thou hast prepared the light and the sun.

In the face of the sun you may see God's beauty ; in the fire you may feel his heat warming ; in the water, his gentleness to refresh you : it is the dew of heaven that makes your field give you bread. — *Taylor.*

2*   c

He giveth snow like wool: he scattereth the hoar-frost like ashes.

He casteth forth his ice like morsels; who can stand before his cold?

He stretcheth out the heavens as a curtain, and spreadeth them out as a tent to dwell in.

Lift up your eyes on high, and behold who hath created these things, that bringeth out their host by number; he calleth them all by names, by the greatness of his might, for that he is strong in power; not one faileth.

The sea is his, and he made it; and his hands formed the dry land.

O Lord, how manifold are thy works! in wisdom hast thou made them all: the earth is full of thy riches.

If the works are so perfect, how glorious must be the Maker of them! If the beauty of that which he has created is inexpressibly great, infinitely greater must be that Being who surveys all creation at a single glance.—*Sturm.*

O come, let us worship and bow down; let us kneel before the Lord our Maker.

Morning.

ALMIGHTY God, may the gift of a new day waken our hearts to new thoughts of love and praise. We thank thee for the continual revelations of thyself through the works of thy hand. The morning is the light of thy smile. The night is the shadow of thy protecting wing. The bounty which supplies our daily returning wants, is the manna which thou dost shower down upon our path. All the gifts of thy Providence are the manifestations of that love which never slumbers nor sleeps. Thou touchest the earth, and it is covered with beauty. Every bush burns with thy presence. Every flower blooms as a fresh token of thy love. Thou settest fast the mountains, and spreadest out the seas as symbols of thy power. Thou crownest the years with thy goodness, and sendest the seed-times and harvests in unbroken succession, to be the constant proofs of thy unchangeable mercy. Heaven and earth show forth thy loving-kindness, and declare thy righteousness.

O God, teach us how to read this book of thy love. Send the spirit of Jesus, thy Son, into our hearts, to open our eyes, and unloose the seals. While we see in the splendors of the firmament the disclosures of thy eternal power and Godhead, may we look upon each lily of the field as a symbol of the love which visits every smallest thing, the grace that waits to bless every humble heart. Give us an ear to hear day unto day uttering speech, and night unto night showing forth the knowledge of thee, until the whole world shall seem to be filled with thy praise.

And yet, O God, while we learn to see thee in thy works, teach us to feel that all this grandeur and beauty cannot fully reveal thy love. The heaven of heavens cannot contain thee. The universe can only give a shadow of thy power and thy mercy. Give to us a perpetual sense of the higher glories of the Holy of Holies, in thy more immediate presence, while we stand here in the outer courts of our Father's house. May the spirit of Him who came to be the express image of thy person, the incarnation of thy love, make us now the sons of God, and prepare us for that higher world where we know not what we shall be, but in which we shall see thee as thou art for evermore.

Hear, forgive, accept us, as disciples of Jesus Christ, our Lord. *Amen.*

EVENING.

O THOU Infinite Spirit, whose creative power and wisdom are revealed in the order and beauty of the universe, filled with grateful wonder at the spectacle of thy works, we worship thee. May our eyes be unsealed to trace more of thy ways in the beneficent arrangements and marvels of nature. And whatever we see of sublimity, loveliness, or blessed adaptation, may it be a symbol to carry our adoring thoughts up to thee. Thus may we walk in the world as in a sacred temple, filled with thy presence, and use all its scenery and phenomena as types and hints through which to commune with the omnipresent Divinity, and discern the indications of his will. We thank thee for the curtain of darkness

thou now lettest down over the slumbers of the
night. Be with our spirits through the hours of
unconsciousness, and restore us to labor and joy of
the day again. And whether we sleep or wake, on
the earth or in worlds unknown, still may we be
thine, thine forever. *Amen.*

I X.

THE VOICE WITHIN.

Hath not thy heart within thee burned
At evening's calm and holy hour,
As if its inmost depths discerned
The presence of a loftier power?

It was the voice of God that spake
In silence to thy silent heart;
And bade each worthier thought awake,
And every dream of earth depart.
                                        BULFINCH.

God never ceases to speak to us; but the noise of the world
without, and the tumult of our passions within, bewilder us,
and prevent us from listening to him. — *Fénelon.*

Blessed is the soul which heareth the Lord speaking within
her, and receiveth from his mouth the word of consolation. —
À Kempis.

Blessed indeed are those ears which listen not after the
voice which is sounding without, but for the truth teaching
inwardly. — *À Kempis.*

Know ye not that ye are the temple of God, and that the Spirit of God dwelleth in you?

God, who commanded the light to shine out of darkness, hath shined in our hearts, to give the light of the knowledge of the glory of God in the face of Jesus Christ.

It is written, Eye hath not seen, nor ear heard, neither hath entered into the heart of man, the things which God hath prepared for them that love him. But God hath revealed them unto us by his Spirit.

For he is our God; and we are the people of his pasture, and the sheep of his hand. To-day if ye will hear his voice, harden not your hearts.

We must often silently listen to this teacher within, who will make known all truth to us, if we are faithful in attending to him.

God is in our souls, as our souls are in our bodies. — *Fénelon.*

And all blessings shall come on thee, and overtake thee, if thou shalt hearken unto the voice of the Lord thy God.

MORNING.

O GOD, our life and our light, the strength of our hearts, the hope of our spirits! We rejoice to know thee, though it be but in part. We desire to know thee more and better, to enter more fully into the joy of thine idea through purity of heart and willing obedience. Flesh and blood hath not revealed thee, but the Light which lighteth all who come into the world is thy witness within us, and the Son who is in the bosom of the Father hath declared thee.

We rejoice in that divine Dispensation of Grace and Truth which shows us the Father, not distant and unheeding, but near to every one of us, and ever willing to help to the uttermost all who seek their help in thee. We bless thee for the word of life in Christ, whereby are given unto us exceeding great and precious promises, and gifts of the Spirit, and means of growth, and aids to virtue. Make that word, we beseech thee, a fountain of strength and healing to our souls ; may it work in us with blessed effect to give us the knowledge of the truth and the power of faith and obedient wills, redeeming us from the law of sin in our members, overcoming every evil tendency and passion, quickening every good principle in our natures, and making us one with God in heart and life.

Make it, we entreat thee, a word of power and life to the nations of the earth, give it the dominion over human ignorance and superstition, over selfish desires, unrighteous laws, and wicked customs, and all the evil that is in the world. May it be not only the message and glad tidings, but the re-alization of peace and good-will on the earth.

Father everlasting ! our hope is in thee ; we wait thy blessing. Grant us of thy mercy whatever in thy wisdom thou shalt see to be needful and fit. Evermore give us of the Bread which cometh down

from heaven and giveth life unto the world, that we
may eat thereof, and not die. Feed our souls, refresh our spirits, strengthen our faith, and lead us
to the Christ to whom he that cometh shall never
hunger, and in whom he that believeth shall
never thirst. And thine be the praise, forevermore. *Amen.*

EVENING.

O THOU, in whom we live and move and have
our being! We are reminded by the experience of another day, that all our ways are ordered
by a loving and compassionate Father. It is the
Spirit itself bearing witness with our spirit that we
are the children of God.

For thy great mercies, thus continually renewed
unto us, we devoutly thank thee. Especially would
we bless and adore thy great and holy name for the
riches of thy goodness in spiritual things ; that thou
hast created us in thine own likeness, and in the image of thine own eternity ; that thou hast revealed
thyself unto us in thy word, and in the thoughts
and affections of our own hearts ; that there is a
voice within, as well as a voice without, calling us
to glory and virtue. May we listen reverently to
the suggestions and warnings of the internal moni-
tor. Suffer us not, we beseech thee, in any moment
of temptation or thoughtlessness, to resist the plead-

ings, the strugglings of our better nature against the besetting sin.

And now we commit ourselves, during the darkness and defencelessness of the hours of sleep, to that ever-watchful Providence which is over all things, ascribing to thee all praise and glory, evermore. *Amen.*

X.

BEARING THE CROSS.

How blessed the man, how fully so,
As far as man is blessed below,
Who, taking up the cross, essays
To follow Jesus all his days.

PARNELL.

And he said unto them all, If any man will come after me, let him deny himself, and take up his cross daily, and follow me.

And he that taketh not his cross, and followeth after me, is not worthy of me.

If thou bear the cross cheerfully, it will bear thee, and lead thee to the desired end, namely, where there shall be an end of suffering, though here there shall not be.— *À Kempis.*

Blessed are ye when men shall revile you and persecute you, and shall say all manner of evil against you falsely for my sake.

Let your light so shine before men that they may see your good works, and glorify your Father which is in heaven.

Whosoever shall confess me before men, him will I confess also before my Father which is in heaven.

By the love of thy cross, O Jesus, I will take up my cross daily and follow thee. — *Bishop Ken.*

I have received the cross, I have received it from thy hand; I will bear it, and bear it even unto death, as thou hast laid it upon me. — *À Kempis.*

I take pleasure in infirmities, in reproaches, in necessities, in persecutions, in distresses for Christ's sake; for when I am weak, then am I strong.

All that will live godly in Christ Jesus shall suffer persecution.

If we suffer, we shall also reign with him : if we deny him, he will also deny us.

He that shall endure unto the end, the same shall be saved.

MORNING.

ALMIGHTY and most merciful God, as once more we gather around the family altar, we would seek thy presence, and invoke thy blessing upon this household. We are weak; wilt thou grant us the aid of thine infinite strength. We are ignorant, and would seek from thine inexhaustible wisdom the light of true knowledge. Borne down with anxiety, with hearts burdened by trial and grief, may we meet the afflictions which beset and surround us with cheerful resignation and unfailing faith. Thou, O Lord, knowest our trials and temptations. We confess our manifold transgressions. When we would do good, evil is present with us. Grant us thy guidance and forgiveness. Sanctify us by thy Holy Spirit. As the shadows of life fall upon our souls, we would seek heavenly light. Without are fightings, within are fears. Enable us, we do most earnestly beseech thee, to bear our cross with lowly submission, uncomplaining fidelity, and serene trust. May we learn from our Saviour to meet our trials with devout confidence and triumphant faith; and cherish the undoubted assurance that a crown of glory awaits the penitent, faithful, and obedient disciple. Though in thy Providence our present lot is grievous; though adversity frown upon us and our bread is dipped in tears; though struggling with a besetting sin or afflicted with sorrow; though subjected to loss of wealth, and, through our fidelity to principle, the esteem of the world, — grant us thy strength, and may we say, in the spirit of Him who bore his agony with such triumphant patience, "Not my will, but thine, be done." May we learn to be resigned even in pain and suffering, and through the pathway of the cross attain unto heavenly glory and divine peace; and thus reap the rich fruition of the believer's faith and the believer's hope. May we both live and die unto Christ, taking up the cross daily, and walk in faithful observance of the precepts of thy Son, Jesus Christ our Lord, —·in the faith of whom, and as whose disciples, we ask for strength and forgiveness. And thine shall be the praise, and the power, and the glory, for ever and ever. *Amen.*

EVENING.

G RACIOUS and Everlasting God, from the distractions and turmoils of the world we turn reverently and solemnly unto thee. And in this hour of quiet meditation would seek our refreshing in that blessed communion which it is our privilege to enjoy.

We thank thee, O our Father, that we may thus come to thee, and that we may indeed believe that thou, the Infinite One, wilt bend to welcome our frail and erring spirits, while they seek direction and strength.

O that our hearts were so in harmony with thy spirit that our communion with thee might be perfect, and that we might know the full blessedness of thy love! Make us, O our Father, more entirely thine. Teach us more and more to realize that there is nothing in heaven or on earth that can bring to us such perfect joy.

·May the image of Jesus be ever present to our thoughts, a constant guide to thee. May we seek to walk ever in his steps. And if they sometimes lead through difficult and trying ways, if sometimes they draw us away from things that we desire, O help us not to falter! What can harm us if we have thy love? And what earthly good shall we not renounce if it turns us away from thee? May we take up our cross and follow Christ, willing even to drink his bitter cup, and to be baptized with his baptism of sorrow, if only we can be found at last with him in thee.

O God, keep us faithful unto death, that we may receive the crown of life. And unto thee, who only art able to keep us from falling, we will ascribe power and dominion, now and for evermore. *Amen.*

XI.

ASPIRATION.

Build thee more stately mansions, O my soul,
As the swift seasons roll!
Leave thy low-vaulted past!
Let each new temple, nobler than the last,
Shut thee from heaven with a dome more vast,
Till thou at length art free,
Leaving thine outgrown shell by life's unresting sea!
HOLMES.

My soul longeth, yea, even fainteth for the courts of the Lord: my heart and my flesh crieth out for the living God.

Let me continue, let me increase in this love of thee more

and more. Let this weary pilgrimage be spent in advancing daily towards thee. — *St. Augustine.*

O God, let thy heavenly love be the constant bias of my soul! May it be the natural spring and weight of my heart, that it may always move towards thee! — *Bishop Ken.*

One thing have I desired of the Lord, that will I seek after; that I may dwell in the house of the Lord all the days of my life, to behold the beauty of the Lord, and to inquire in his temple.

Blessed are they which do hunger and thirst after righteousness, for they shall be filled.

Teach me, O Lord, the way of thy statutes; and I shall keep it unto the end.

Give me understanding, and I shall keep thy law; yea, I shall observe it with my whole heart.

Behold, I have longed after thy precepts; quicken me in thy righteousness.

I will delight myself in thy statutes: I will not forget thy word.

Blessed are they that dwell in thy house; they will be still praising thee.

They go from strength to strength; every one of them in Zion appeareth before God.

Grow in grace, and in the knowledge of our Lord and Saviour Jesus Christ. To him be glory both now and forever.

MORNING.

INFINITE Being, in whom all perfections meet, send thy Spirit down to lift our spirits up to thee. We would not grovel on the low level of time and sense, contented with things that perish. We would aspire evermore from height to height, through knowledge and trust, through obedience and love, still rising, till we reach our perfection. We thank thee for the sacred lures thou dost hold above us, to tempt our desires aloft. O may we forget the things which are below, and press forwards and upwards towards the mark for the prize of our high calling in Christ Jesus. Lessen the attraction of ignoble things, and increase the power of all forms of celestial good to draw our souls to themselves. Especially, O God, reveal the glories of thine own being, the loveliness of thine own face to us, that, turning from all else, we may supremely strive to win and lose ourselves in thee. Pardon us, and bless us, O thou who in all and over all art God alone. *Amen.*

Evening.

HOLY Father, maker of the countless worlds above us, former of our bodies, God of our lives, and Father of our spirits, — as thy angel of the night closes the day here on earth, the gates of thy boundless kingdom open over our heads, and call our thoughts upward to commune with Him who inhabiteth immensity. Lord of the shining ones, Guide of all who pass through these lowly

scenes of tribulation toward the realms of glory and
the city of peace, shine down to-night into our
hearts, and kindle in us a renewed yearning and an
effectual purpose to put off utterly the works of
darkness and clothe ourselves in the armor of light.
The day of God is at hand ; O may we be children
of the day, may we behold the ladder set up on the
earth, the top whereof reacheth heaven, and may
we climb by the steps of memory and hope and
prayer and patience toward that perfection which
beams upon us in all thy works and ways, and of
which this night, with all its wonders and gracious
whisperings, affords us such blessed intimations. As
night after night admonishes us of the time when
this earthly house must be dissolved, may the inner
man be built up day after day. This is not our rest.

Forgetting the things which are behind and below,
we would press on to those which are above. O,
may this night's slumber refresh us for a nobler renewal of the race which is set before us in Christ
Jesus ! May our loins be ever girded about, and our
lamps trimmed and burning ; may neither the weari-
ness of the flesh, nor the world's cares or pleasures,
deaden our zeal for the prize of our high calling ;
may we be made more than conquerors through the
Captain of our salvation, and by patient continuance
in well-doing attain to glory, honor, and immortality.
Amen.

XII.

GOOD RESOLUTIONS.

May I resolve, with all my heart,
With all my powers, to serve the Lord ,
Nor from his precepts e'er depart,
Whose service is a rich reward.

MRS. STEELE.

Be not rash with thy mouth, and let not thine heart be hasty to utter anything before God; for God is in heaven, and thou art upon earth : therefore let thy words be few.

When thou vowest a vow unto God, defer not to pay it ; for he hath no pleasure in fools ; pay that which thou hast vowed.

I will behave myself wisely in a perfect way. I will walk within my house with a perfect heart.

I will set no wicked thing before mine eyes: I hate the work of them that turn aside ; it shall not cleave to me.

God never accepts a good inclination instead of a good action, where that action may be done. — *South.*

I find a law, that, when I would do good, evil is present with me.

Watch ye, stand fast in the faith, be strong.

Let us hold fast the profession of our faith without wavering ; for he is faithful that promised.

I have sworn, and I will perform it, that I will keep thy righteous judgments.

There wants nothing but a believing prayer to turn a promise into a performance. — *J. Mason.*

Godliness consists not in a heart to intend to do the will of
God, but in a heart to do it. — *Jonathan Edwards.*

First know what is good to be done, then do that good, being
known. — *Warwick.*

Now thanks be unto God, which always causeth us to triumph in Christ.

MORNING.

GOD of the morning, who makest its outgoings
to rejoice! We thank thee for thy bounty,
which now with the light of the sun reneweth the
face of the earth. May thy celestial light shine in
upon our souls, and renew in them all holy feelings
and virtuous resolutions. We begin the day with
thee, O God; grant us to spend it in thy fear and
love. May we with thoughtful minds survey the
path which lies before us, perceive to what moral
dangers we may be most exposed therein, and arm
ourselves with strong determination that we will
avoid every action, every word, and every volun-
tary thought, contrary to thy will and to our duty.
In humility would we profess our purpose unto thee,
to exercise due restraint over each appetite and
passion that rebels against the sway of reason and
of religion. We would resolve before thee to apply
ourselves to the steady and cheerful performance
of those common tasks which thy providence has

assigned to us; and to do with our might whatever our hands find to do, whereby thy children may be aided and thy name be glorified. And if our duties, this day, or at any time to come, should be less of action than of endurance, then would we resolve, O Father, bravely and meekly to endure, remembering how the blessed Jesus bore the burden of pain, reproach, and sorrow for our sakes. O thou in whose presence these purposes are formed and expressed, we know that our strength is but weakness without thine aid. Give us of thy grace, O Lord! and make us conquerors through the spirit of him that loved us and gave himself for us. As we have prayed for ourselves, we pray for others; those who are near us as relatives and friends, and those who are afar off, even all mankind. At length, O Father, of thy mercy, make us thine in heaven. And to thy name be praises evermore, through Christ our Lord. *Amen.*

EVENING.

O THOU all-searching and everywhere-present God, we pray that we may both know and see ourselves as thou knowest and seest us. We are now before thee, with our hearts open to the gaze of thy all-penetrating eye. As in thy presence we review the past day, we have need to be truly penitent, for we have often done those things which we

ought not to have done, and we have left undone
those things which we ought to have done. In
word, in deed, and in thought, we have offended
against thy most holy law. We are imperfect in
thy sight. We feel our need of a new and better
life. But in our imperfection and need we remember that thy law is perfect, converting the soul; thy
commandments are pure, enlightening the eyes; thy
judgments are true and righteous altogether. Let
sin have no dominion over us; cleanse us from
secret faults; keep back thy servants from presumptuous sins, and let them have no dominion over us.
But even while our sins are before us we remember
thy promises. Grant us the aid of thy Holy Spirit.
May the conviction of our past transgressions quick-
en within us holier resolutions, and lead us to a
more complete consecration of our hearts to thee.
Through the power of an awakened conscience
may we be quickened to greater vigilance in the
performance of every duty, and aim to give our
lives to thee, which is our reasonable and acceptable
service. All that we have and all that we are
belong to thee. May we resolve with all our hearts
to employ them in thy service, and to faithfully
strive to do thy most perfect will. Strengthen
within us devout purposes, and increase our aspirations after holiness. Thou, O God, wilt call us
to a strict account for the use of every day. May
we so walk in the way of thy statutes, and keep thy

commandments, as to meet with thine approval, and live day by day with the blessed assurance that for thy faithful and obedient children there awaiteth a crown of glory and everlasting peace, through our Lord and Saviour, Jesus Christ. *Amen.*

XIII.

THY KINGDOM COME.

Thy kingdom come, with power and grace,
To every heart of man ;
Thy peace and joy and righteousness
In all our bosoms reign.
WESLEY'S COLL.

And when he was demanded of the Pharisees, when the kingdom of God should come, he answered them and said, The kingdom of God cometh not with observation :

Neither shall they say, Lo here ! or, Lo there ! for, behold, the kingdom of God is within you.

The kingdom of heaven is like unto leaven, which a woman took and hid in three measures of meal till the whole was leavened.

Again, the kingdom of heaven is like unto treasure hid in a field ; the which when a man hath found he hideth, and for joy thereof goeth and selleth all that he hath, and buyeth the field.

Again, the kingdom of heaven is like unto a merchantman
seeking goodly pearls :

Who, when he had found one pearl of great price, went and
sold all that he had, and bought it.

Thy kingdom is an everlasting kingdom, and thy dominion
endureth throughout all generations.

For the earth shall be filled with the knowledge of the glory
of the Lord, as the waters cover the sea.

All the ends of the world shall remember and turn unto the
Lord ; and all the kindreds of the nations shall worship before
thee.

For the kingdom is the Lord's, and he is governor among
the nations.

Then shall the earth yield her increase ; and God, even our
own God, shall bless us :

When the people are gathered together, and the kingdoms,
to serve the Lord.

Morning.

O THOU, who reignest in the heaven of heavens, and whose dominion is over all the earth,
we bow in reverence before thine infinite majesty,
and acknowledge our humble allegiance to thee.
We know that in thy service is our highest good,
and that thy perfect government is the true life
to the soul. But, O God, we confess our proneness
to break away from thee and do violence to thy
commands ; and we fervently pray that thou wilt

bring us back and keep us in loving subjection to thy holy will.

O that our hearts might be opened so to comprehend thy infinite perfections that thou shouldest truly reign over us as the object of our adoring love. O that we might learn the beauty and glory of thy holiness and truth, which it is given even to us, creatures of frailty and sin, yet also children of thy love, to strive after and to share. Do thou grant that so, filled with a sense of thy excellence and a yearning for the things of God, our hearts may be indeed thy throne, and our members all ministers to do thy will.

And O may thy kingdom come, not only in us, but in all the world. Thou only canst fill and satisfy the vast capacities wherewith thou hast endowed the human soul. Suffer not thy erring children to wander far away from thee and goodness in disobedience and wrong, and to give themselves to the unsatisfying dominion of worldly lusts. But may the divine power of thy truth and holiness be victorious over every evil principle, and thy will rule within us a living spring and guide.

May the time be no longer when thou shalt say, " If I be a father, where is mine honor ? if I be a master, where is my fear ? " But do thou reign, whose right it is, and in whose service is happiness and joy and peace.

We ask it as disciples of our Lord Jesus Christ. *Amen.*

EVENING.

OUR Father, who art in heaven, thou whose strength is upholding us, and whose love is descending upon us every day, we come unto thee at this evening hour with the grateful offerings of our hearts. Wilt thou listen to our prayer, and graciously accept us in the sacrifice we bring before thee. We thank thee for the care with which thou hast kept us during another period of our probation, for the bounty with which thou hast supplied our returning wants, and for the opportunities which thou hast afforded us for a wise and useful improvement of our time. Enable us to feel, O God, that all the blessings of life come from thee; and in our enjoyment of them may our hearts ever turn with grateful emotions to thee. Forgive us, we beseech thee, if we have been unmindful of thee in receiving thy gifts, and wherein we have sinned against thee in our waywardness or our ignorance.

O God, our Heavenly Father, we pray for the coming of thy kingdom; that kingdom which Christ Jesus our Lord came to set up here on earth to be for evermore in the hearts of thy children. Our heart's desire and prayer is, that all mankind may come to a knowledge of the truth, and by the truth may be set free from the bondage of the world and the bondage of sin; and that thy grace may dwell in all richly, and thy spirit sanctify their spirits, and so thy kingdom come to be established throughout the world. O our Father, we would ourselves be the subjects of thy kingdom. We would be sharers with all our fellow-men in that peace and joy and righteousness which it so abundantly imparts. To this end we would ever come to thee, to be enlightened by thy wisdom, and to be renewed in the spirit of our minds by thy Holy Spirit abiding within us. O God, our help is in thee, and from thee cometh our salvation; and we feel assured that thou wilt keep thy promise unto us and to all men; the promise that if we ask, we shall receive; if we seek, we shall find; if we knock, it shall be opened unto us.

O our Father, hear our prayer, we beseech thee, and grant the desires of our hearts, and thine shall be the glory and the praise forevermore. *Amen.*

3*

XIV.

A PATIENT, FORGIVING SPIRIT.

Wouldst thou, when thy faults are known,
Wish that pardon should be shown ?
Be forgiving, then, and do
As thou wouldst be done unto.

W. ROSCOE.

Endeavor to be patient in bearing with the defects and infirmities of others, of what sort soever they be ; for that thyself also hast many failings which must be borne with by others. — *À Kempis.*

He shall have judgment without mercy that hath shown no mercy.

Hath any wronged thee ? be bravely revenged ; slight it, and the work is begun ; forgive it, and it is finished. — *Quarles.*

If ye forgive men their trespasses, your Heavenly Father will also forgive your trespasses.

You who complain so much of what others make you suffer, do you think that you cause others no pain ? Does it never come into your mind to fear, lest he should demand of you why you had not exercised towards your brother a little of that mercy which he who is your Master so abundantly bestows upon you ? — *Fénelon.*

Let no malice or ill-will abide in me. Give me grace to forgive all that may have offended me. — *Wilson.*

Blessed are the merciful, for they shall obtain mercy.

When ye stand praying, forgive, if ye have aught against

any : that your Father also which is in heaven may forgive you your trespasses.

Comfort the feeble-minded, support the weak, be patient toward all men. See that none render evil for evil unto any man.

Seest thou a man that is hasty in his words ? there is more hope of a fool than of him.

Be ye kind one to another, tender-hearted, forgiving one another, even as God for Christ's sake hath forgiven you.

MORNING.

O THOU, who makest the outgoings of the morning to rejoice, we thank thee that we are permitted again to see the pleasant light, and to enjoy and admire thy glorious and wonderful works. What are we, that thou shouldest visit us every night and morning with blessings more than can be numbered ! That thou shouldest watch over us in our sleep, and smile on us when we wake, and hold us up in all our ways ! That thou shouldest spread our table and fill our cup ; provide for us the comforts of an earthly home, and cheer us with the promise of a heavenly ! O, may thine unmerited goodness lead us to a sincere repentance, and kindle in our hearts such fervent love as will make us watchful not to offend or grieve thy Holy Spirit, and ever ready to do and bear thy perfect will. May it soften our hearts also towards our fellow-men, and dispose us to compassion and forgiveness.

As thou art so long-suffering towards us, may we exercise patience and forbearance towards others. May the consciousness of our own faults lead us to regard theirs with pity, and judge them with charity. Since our goodness cannot extend unto thee, may it be extended, for thy sake, to thy children who are around us. While the light of thy countenance is shining upon us, may it be our delight to reflect it upon them. When thou increasest our store, let us multiply our benefactions, — wasting nothing upon our selfishness, and perverting nothing to luxury and pride; but using and enjoying everything for the diffusion of happiness and the advancement of thy glory. This day may we be followers of Christ, by walking in love, and going about doing good; by cultivating a meek and patient spirit, and maintaining a forgiving and placable temper; by seeking rather to minister than to be ministered unto, and remembering in our practice his precious saying, " It is more blessed to give than to receive."

Accept, O Lord, our intercessions for all mankind; especially for the poor and the sick, the desolate and the fallen, the weary and heavy-laden.

And now, O holy and merciful Father, we humbly commend unto thy gracious care ourselves and all who are dear to us. Guard and guide us through all the unknown scenes and dangers of the day. Assist us to discharge faithfully every

duty, and to bear patiently every trial ; to trust
in thee with a childlike confidence, and to please
and glorify thee in all our doings. And to thee,
the infinite and eternal God, we will ascribe continually all glory, honor, and praise, through Jesus
Christ our Lord. *Amen.*

EVENING.

O LORD our God! look on us in love, as we
commend ourselves to thee at the close of this
day. We acknowledge that thy hand has been
open to feed us ; and that streams of mercy, never
ceasing, have flowed to us from thine exhaustless
fountains. O Lord! thou art kind to the un-
thankful and the evil ; for thou hast been kind to
us. Thou hast sought us when we wandered ;
thou hast remembered us when we forgot thee ;
thou hast been patient with our infirmities, and
ready to forgive our sins ; and all thy chastisements
have been for our profit. May thy goodness lead
us to humble repentance ; may it waken in us an
earnest desire to be like thee in our lives, and to
deal with our fellow-servants as thou hast dealt with
us. Fill us with thine own heavenly spirit of good-
will ; give us a tender, Christ-like interest in the
welfare of all thy human family ; and may the sins
and errors of mankind move us to compassionate
efforts for their redemption. Help us to amend our

own lives and to correct our own faults, that we may be more fitting instruments and examples of good to others.

Father! may we lie down to rest with hearts at peace with thee and with all thy creatures. May the remainder of our days be spent more wisely than the past. And when the shadows of death shall darken our mortal sight, may our faith be cheered with the dawning visions of eternal day. And to thee will we give endless praises, as our God and Father, and the God and Father of our Lord Jesus Christ. *Amen.*

XV.

THE CHRISTIAN LIFE A WARFARE.

A soldier's course, from battles won,
To new-commencing strife;
A pilgrim's, restless as the sun; —
Behold the Christian's life!
GISBORNE.

Think not that I am come to send peace on earth; I came not to send peace, but a sword.

Put on the whole armor of God, that ye may be able to stand against the wiles of the devil.

This charge I commit unto thee, that thou mightest war a good warfare;

Holding faith and a good conscience; which some having put away, concerning faith have made shipwreck.

But then follow after righteousness, godliness, faith, love, patience, meekness.

Fight the good fight of faith, lay hold on eternal life.

Be strong in the grace that is in Christ Jesus.

Therefore endure hardness, as a good soldier of Jesus Christ.

No man that warreth entangleth himself with the affairs of this life; that he may please him who hath chosen him to be a soldier.

And if a man also strive for masteries, yet is he not crowned except he strive lawfully.

The weapons of our warfare are not carnal, but mighty through God to the pulling down of strong holds; —

Casting down imaginations, and every high thing that exalteth itself against the knowledge of God, and bringing into captivity every thought to the obedience of Christ.

No triumphs are comparable to those of piety, — no trophies so magnificent and durable as those which victorious faith erecteth. — *Barrow.*

MORNING.

OUR Father, who art in heaven, and our God; awakened to the light of another day, we come to thee with the grateful offerings of our hearts. We thank thee, O God, for the continuance of our lives, and the renewal of our energies; and for the freshness and vigor with which we are enabled to go forth again to our labors and our duties.

As this day upon which we have entered shall be to each one of us, so let our strength be, we beseech thee, O our Father. As we shall be beset by sins, and shall meet with temptations, wilt thou aid us by thy heavenly grace in overcoming and resisting them. If hard trials and experiences await us ; if disappointments and afflictions shall fall to our lot ; if heavy burdens shall be laid upon us, — give us wisdom, we beseech thee, to see thy hand in them, and by thy Holy Spirit in our hearts breathe into us the spirit of devout submission.

O our Father! we feel that we are weak and ignorant and sinful ; but thou art holy and just and good. Our trust is in thee ; our hope is in thee. We know that, if we seek help of thee, thou wilt give us help according to our needs ; for this assurance we have from our Lord and Saviour Jesus Christ ; and that thou wilt not suffer us to be overcome and cast down in our conflicts in this world, but wilt make them the means by which our strength shall be renewed and our faith deepened, and so by them we shall day by day be prepared for the great warfare in which we are called to engage.

Do thou be with us all this day, our Heavenly Father, our defence and our salvation in every hour of danger and of evil. If consistent with thy holy will, do thou preserve us from sickness and suffering and sorrow. We entreat thy blessing for our friends, and for all who are near and dear to us. Do thou keep them, and lead them by thy wisdom into all righteousness and truth and peace.

And we pray, O God, that thy kingdom may come and thy will may be done here on earth even as it is done in heaven. And thine shall be the praise and the glory now and evermore. *Amen.*

EVENING.

ALMIGHTY God, thy power and love have been over us during the busy hours of the day, while we were engaged in the duties and enjoyments of active life. May the thought of thy continued presence hallow all our other thoughts, blending with all that we say and all that we do, making our labor prayer, and our happiness thanksgiving. Wilt thou strengthen us every day for the work that thou givest us to do. If it be arduous, may we take courage from the prize of our high calling, and the hope that is full of immortality. If it require self-denial, may we look to the cross, and drink in the spirit of the Crucified. Wilt thou arm us against the temptations that may beset our path. Let not appetite or passion, low desire or unworthy love, make us forgetful of our divine sonship, and of the glorious destiny that awaits him who is faithful unto the end. May we take to ourselves the weapons of our Saviour's warfare;

E

may we pray with all diligence, and watch con
stantly against evil, and thus may we come off more
than conquerors. And not only may we resist the
allurements of sin, may we feel that incessant progress is at once our sacred duty and our blessed
privilege ; that, if we indeed belong to Christ, we
must be his close and ever closer followers; and
that our assurance of heavenly happiness can be
made firm and clear only by having all our steps
on earth tend heavenward. May we keep in mind
the frailty of life and the possible nearness of death ;
and wilt thou grant us grace so to live that to die
shall be gain. Take us under thy merciful care this
night.

Bless, with us, those whom thou hast given us.
May they all be thine ; and may every tie of kindred and affection be made the stronger and the
dearer by Christian sympathy and a common interest in the great salvation. We commend to thee
the poor, sick, and suffering ; those in error, ignorance, and sin ; those who know not thee and obey
not thy Gospel. May thy kingdom come, and thy
will be done on earth as it is done in heaven ; for
thine is the kingdom, the power, and the glory
forever. *Amen.*

XVI.

DEPENDENCE UPON GOD.

Man's wisdom is to seek
His strength in God alone;
And e'en an angel would be weak,
Who trusted in his own.
                              COWPER.

There is no sanctity, if thou, O Lord, withdraw thine hand.

No wisdom availeth, if thou cease to guide;

No courage helpeth, if thou leave off to defend;

No chastity is secure, if thou do not protect it;

No custody of our own availeth, if thy sacred watchfulness be not present with us. — *À Kempis.*

Fear thou not; for I am with thee: be not dismayed; for I am thy God: I will strengthen thee; yea, I will help thee; yea, I will uphold thee.

The Lord is my rock, and my fortress, and my deliverer; my God, and my strength, in whom I will trust; my buckler, and the horn of my salvation, and my high tower.

In him we live and move and have our being.

There is no wisdom, nor understanding, nor counsel, against the Lord.

I can do nothing without the help of God, and that even from moment to moment. — *St. Athanasius.*

The horse is prepared against the day of battle; but safety is of the Lord.

Though I walk in the midst of trouble, thou wilt revive me.

The beloved of the Lord shall dwell in safety; and the Lord shall cover him all the day long.

I will both lay me down in peace, and sleep; for thou, Lord, makest me dwell in safety.

MORNING.

ALMIGHTY Father, again thy hand has lifted up the sun and restored us from sleep and dreams to thoughts of duty and the cares of our worldly business. It is thou that hast done it. We devoutly acknowledge our dependence on thee. Without the air we should gasp and die, and without thy spirit we should instantly become nothing. Thou art the life and law of all. We desire to be ever mindful of this solemn truth. O aid us, great God, to return in love and service, by obedience to thy commands, and kind deeds to our fellow-creatures, the unfailing gifts thou pourest on us. Let a sense of our pervading dependence on thy Spirit deepen our lives, and lead us more earnestly to meditate on thy requirements and consecrate ourselves to thy will. We pray to thee in the name of Jesus. O, hear our prayer, and answer it according to thine infinite wisdom and goodness. *Amen.*

EVENING.

THOU, O Father, of whose goodness another day has been added to our lives, art still with us as a friend and protector. Accept the thanksgiving which now, with united heart, we offer to thee with our evening devotions. For all our thoughts of peace, this day, we bless thee. For the strength which has been given us to use, and for the means which have been placed in our hands, we acknowledge our dependence upon thee. The day is thine and the night also. The cold and the heat, the seed-time and the harvest, are thine. From thee are bestowed all the good gifts by which our lives are sustained, and by which our home is made comfortable and happy. For these, and for the friends whom we can so fully love and trust, and for the instructions which guide us in the way of knowledge and duty, we thank thee, Almighty Father.

May we have great comfort and peace in the thought that *in thee* do we live and move and have our being. May we be so at one with thyself that thine own holy purposes may indeed be accomplished in all the various changes of our lives, and in every allotment of prosperity or adversity. May we so completely submit ourselves, and all we have, to thy disposal, that we may have no fear of evil while we do thy will.

Thou knowest, O God, the imperfection of our understanding, and the frailty of our good resolves. But, in thy mercy, wilt thou pardon our ignorance and sin. And, according to thy blessed promises, make thou our strength equal to our duty, and give us wisdom in proportion to our need. *Amen.*

———

XVII.

PURITY.

Immortal man, keep pure
Thyself, that mystic shrine;
Let hate of all that's dark endure,
And love of all divine.
                         JOHNS.

He that loveth pureness of heart, for the grace of his lips the king shall be his friend.

Blessed are the pure in heart, for they shall see God.

Every man that hath this hope in him purifieth himself, even as He is pure.

If we did certainly believe that we were members of Christ, and God's temples, how should we but flee from all impurity and corruption of the world. — *John Bradford.*

Dearly beloved, I beseech you as strangers and pilgrims, abstain from fleshly lusts, which war against the soul.

Who shall ascend into the hill of the Lord? or who shall stand in his holy place? —

He that hath clean hands, and a pure heart; who hath not lifted up his soul unto vanity, nor sworn deceitfully.

Who can say I have made my heart clean, I am pure from my sin?

Draw nigh unto God, and he will draw nigh unto you. Cleanse your hands and purify your hearts.

Lord, if thou wilt, thou canst make me clean.

Wash me thoroughly from mine iniquity, and cleanse me from my sin.

Let us draw near with a true heart, in full assurance of faith, having our hearts sprinkled from an evil conscience, and our bodies washed with pure water.

Let us consider one another, to provoke unto love and to good works.

MORNING.

O THOU infinitely pure and holy God, we, thy dependent children, bless thee for the gift of a new day. We desire to humble ourselves in thy pure and perfect sight. The secrets of our hearts are known to thee. Thou seest every hidden frailty, every impurity in our affections and desires. Reveal to us these stains upon our souls. Save us from examining ourselves by poor and worldly standards, and lift our eyes to that perfect law which discerns the thoughts and intents of the heart. Let us never be content until we hear its sentence against our open and secret sins.

O God, unworthy as we are, how can we truly
serve and worship thee? We ask for a greater
sincerity in all our prayers. Save us from wandering thoughts; from coldness of heart. May every
supplication be a deep cry of the soul for pardon
and help. Give us a greater singleness of purpose
every day in the work which thou givest us to do.
Make it our constant aim to do thy will. Remove
the selfishness from our breasts. Make our chari-
ties sincere. Let them not be the unwilling offerings of the hands, but the free outpourings of love.
Guard the temple of our hearts against the entrance
of impure and evil thoughts. Close our ears against
every whisper of envy, of uncharitableness, of pride,
and rebuke every imagination which can defile our
inmost soul.

O Father, we can do nothing without thy help.
Fix our affections upon thee, and then we shall be
raised above the temptations of worldly thoughts.
Turn us with all the heart towards thy truth, and
evil will flee away. Create within us the spirit
of our Master and Lord, and then may we walk
securely through his divine strength. Almighty
God, hear our earnest prayers, and never leave nor
forsake us till thou hast cleansed the deepest springs
of· life, and made every thought and desire acceptable to thee. We ask and offer all as disciples
of thy dear Son, and through him to thee ascribe
the glory and the praise. *Amen.*

Evening.

PAREN'T of our soul, who hast made it innocent, modest, and pure, keep it as thou hast
made it, or purify it, and make it again as thou
wouldest have it kept. We are thy temple: may
we not defile thy temple. May no low desires,
impure passions, kill out the life of our soul. May
not earthly love poison heavenly love: may not
the lower love, snare of the feet, seeming joy
but real anguish, clouding the generous thought,
dulling the bright eye, making heavy the youth-
ful face,—may it not get possession over us. O,
do thou help us to keep under the body, and
bring it into subjection, that we may not be cast-
aways.

But rather, Father, lift our thoughts to chaste
and noble aims, purify our souls to the best desires; if it be necessary, try us with purifying fire,
as silver is tried, till all dross pass away. Fill our
minds with noble thoughts, teach us to despise luxury, self-indulgence, and sin ; teach us to rise nearer
to thee. May the purity of Christ's soul inspire our
souls, and lead us away from disgraceful passions,
which dishonor our names, and cloud our influence,
and disturb our homes, and kill our hearts. Let
heaven conquer earth within us, God conquer
sense and sin, life triumph over all decay and death.
As Christ our master walked in holiness and in all

4

sweet, serene affections, so may we walk calm in true and good thoughts, delivered from the power of all evil, which we ask in Him. . *Amen.*

XVIII.

CHRIST THE WAY.

Thou art the way, — and he who sighs,
  Amid this starless waste of wo,
To find a pathway to the skies,
  A light from heaven's eternal glow,
By thee must come, thou gate of love,
  Through which the saints undoubting trod;
Till faith discovers, like the dove,
  An ark, a resting-place in God.
                                        ANON.

Jesus saith, I am the way, the truth, and the life; no man cometh unto the Father but by me.

Go where thou wilt, seek whatsoever thou wilt, thou shalt not find a higher way above, nor a safer way below, than the way of the holy Cross. — *À Kempis.*

One ray of moral and religious truth is worth all the wisdom of the schools. One lesson from Christ will carry you higher than years of study under those who are too enlightened to follow this celestial guide. — *Channing.*

This is a faithful saying, and worthy of all acceptation, that Christ Jesus came into the world to save sinners.

Though he were a Son, yet learned he obedience by the things which he suffered; and being made perfect, he became the author of eternal salvation unto all them that obey him.

For other foundation can no man lay than is laid, which is Jesus Christ.

Jesus spake, saying, I am the light of the world: he that followeth me shall not walk in darkness, but shall have the light of life.

Teach me thy way, O Lord, and lead me in a plain path.

Jesus said, I am come a light into the world, that whosoever believeth on me should not abide in darkness.

He that rejecteth me and receiveth not my words, hath one that judgeth him: the word that I have spoken, the same shall judge him in the last day.

For it had been better not to have known the way of righteousness, than, after having known it, to turn from the holy commandment.

MORNING.

O THOU Almighty and Eternal God, who dwellest in light inaccessible and full of glory, we thank thee that thou dost visit thy children not alone in the outward light of day which is now shining around us, but that thou dost come to us more nearly and reveal thyself to us more clearly in him who is the way of truth and life. Lord, we believe in him; help thou our unbelief. Help us to draw nigh to him and to commit ourselves entirely to his guidance. May we be ready to leave all and follow him, walking securely because we walk with him. As we commune with him, may our hearts be touched and made better, renewed and sanctified by thy spirit. May he be to us the way, the truth, and the life, and, through his influence upon us, may the day which is now begun be a blessing to every one of us, and help us faithfully to fulfil all its duties. Bind us more tenderly to our friends. Cherish within us holy affections and desires, and lead us on in the way which he hath trod, to that world on which no morning sun shall rise, .for the glory of the Lord doth lighten it, and the lamb is the light thereof. In his name, and by his disciples, we ask and offer all. And thine be the kingdom and the power and the glory, for ever and ever. *Amen.*

EVENING.

HOLY Father, now the day is done and the shadows of night are falling around us, we would bow before thee in grateful recognition of thy guidance and care. We would call home our thoughts from the duties, labors, and pleasures in which we have been engaged, and fix them in reverent contemplation of our Divine Master. We need to correct our life, our thought, our heart, daily, by that holy pattern. We would set its blessed likeness in our souls, that our daily going may have its constant presence and gentle admonition. O God, we know the truth of thy Son, his blessed life, his childlike obedience, his unwearying toil, his holy patience and tender love. These are the way of the godly life to us, and may we be taught by thy Spirit, and by the experience of our own hearts, that this is our true life. Teach us that when we are away from Christ, we are away from our better selves, and away from thee. Help us to look back upon the day which has closed, that our hearts may have humiliation or devout gratitude, according as we have humbly sought to follow in our Master's footsteps ; and inspire us, O God, with devout and holy purpose to follow thy dear Son with renewed mind and heart. May the love wherewith thou hast loved us in him lead us continually to penitence and contrition, that thy Spirit may dwell in us, and our life be hid with Christ in God. Thus may we find that living unto thee is life indeed, and that our Lord is the way of that life.

Come unto us now in thy gracious compassion, and let us lie down in holy confidence and trust, for whether we wake, or whether we sleep, we are still with thee. *Amen.*

XIX.

THE WISE CHOICE.

May I resolve with all my heart,
With all my powers, to serve the Lord ;
Nor from his precepts e'er depart,
Whose service is a rich reward.
MRS. STEELE.

Choose ye this day whom ye will serve.

Call upon the name of the Lord, to serve him with one consent.

Whom have I in heaven but thee, O Lord? and there is none on earth that I desire beside thee.

Thou art my God and I will thank thee; thou art my God, and I will serve thee.

I will abide in thy tabernacle forever; I will trust in the covert of thy wings.

To be silent, to suffer, to pray when we cannot act, is acceptable to God. A disappointment, a contradiction, a harsh word received and endured as in his presence, is worth more than a long prayer. — *Fénelon.*

Return, and discern between the righteous and the wicked, between him that serveth God, and him that serveth him not.

By faith Moses, when he was come to years, refused to be called the son of Pharaoh's daughter; choosing rather to suffer affliction with the people of God, than to enjoy the pleasures of sin for a season.

O welcome service and ever to be desired, in which we are rewarded with the Greatest Good, and attain to joy which shall endlessly remain with us. — *À Kempis.*

Know thou the God of thy father, and serve him with a perfect heart and with a willing mind. If thou seek him, he will be found of thee.

As a man, thou hast nothing to commend thee to thyself, but that only by which thou art a man; that is, by what thou choosest and refusest. — *Taylor.*

Hear instruction and be wise, and refuse it not.

Whoso hearkeneth unto me shall dwell safely, and shall be quiet from fear of evil.

MORNING.

ALMIGHTY God, our merciful Father, we thank thee that thou hast heard our prayers, and hast blessed us with thy protection as the night went by. And now that a new day begins, — and we enter upon its duties, — we ask the same protection, and the same blessing. Be pleased to remember us, though we forget thee ; be pleased to show us how we can make good the resolutions of yesterday ; be pleased to show us what thou wouldst have us to do this day, that we may live to thy praise, as in the prayers and meditations of yesterday we have promised. Help us to choose the good, the true, the pure, and reject the evil.

We ask thy blessing also upon all whom we love, who are not here with us. Be pleased to smile on all the other homes which are very dear to us, and teach us all that we are close together when we come to thee.

We pray for our country, for thy holy Church everywhere, and for all our brethren and sisters of mankind.

In the name of the Lord Jesus, our Saviour. *Amen.*

EVENING.

OUR Heavenly Father, the labors of the day are ended, and in thy loving providence we are drawing near to the hours of rest. We seek the shelter of thine arms. When we are sinking into unconsciousness, we feel more than ever that we live encompassed by mystery, and that we can only trust in the All-wise and the All-merciful. Father, let there be nothing between our souls and thee. We would surrender our all, our most precious treasure, into the keeping of the mighty and gracious God. If we are keeping back anything, may we keep it back no longer! In times past, we have too often brought unto thee only half our hearts and half our possessions, and so we have had no peace; and when the shades of night have gathered about us, we have been cast down, and disquieted, and fearful, we have taken anxious thought for the morrow, and have not gloried in our cross, or rejoiced in the fellowship of the Lord's sufferings. Save us henceforth, dear Father, from our foolishness and our wickedness! May we choose thee for our portion, and the life of thy dear Son for our life, that we may have him with us henceforth in the house of feasting and the house of mourning, and break bread with him in the kingdom of God which he has established on earth. O Lord, we know that if we keep back anything it is to our great loss ; that if in one point we fail in trusting loyalty, we fail in all; knowing these things, may we do them! Come, O thou guiding and gracious Spirit, and fill, warm, and satisfy our hearts! May our eyes be open to behold thee, the Supreme Beauty. Too late have we learned to love thee, and yet not too late, for thou art infinite in compassion and wonderful in all thy ways, and thou regardest not the sinner of yesterday, but the penitent and loving child who seeks thee now, prostrate at the feet of the ever-blessed Mediator. O dear God and Father, make us wholly thine! May we love no child, no creature, of thine, save in thee, O Thou who art infinitely lovely, the Beginning and End of all perfection! Let thy hand rest upon us! From thy hand none shall be able to pluck us! May we love thee! May we have this proof of thy love, and that thou hast called us, and that nothing henceforth shall be able to separate us from thee! So, Father, may we live and die! It is our prayer in Him who never did his own will, or sought his own glory. *Amen.*

XX.

RETIREMENT AND MEDITATION.

By all means use sometimes to be alone,
Salute thyself; see what thy soul doth wear,
Dare to look in thy chest; for 't is thine own;
And tumble up and down what thou find'st there.
Who cannot rest till he good fellows finde,
He breaks up house, turns out of doors his mind.

HERBERT.

It is not hasty reading, but seriously meditating upon holy and heavenly truths, that makes them prove sweet and profitable to the soul. — *Bishop Hall.*

How vain to excite in our hearts sacred and holy emotions, unless we are afterwards careful to close the outlet by diligent reflection and prayer, and so preserve it unspotted from the world. — *Anon.*

Commune with your own heart upon your bed, and be still.

I will meditate on thy precepts, and have respect unto thy ways.

When thou prayest, enter into thy closet, and when thou hast shut the door, pray to thy Father which is in secret; and thy Father which seeth in secret shall reward thee openly.

Thou art my hiding-place and my shield; I hope in thy word.

Every person holds an inward conversation with himself which it highly concerns him well to regulate, because, even in this sense, evil conversations corrupt good manners. — *Pascal.*

Blessed is the man that walketh not in the counsel of the ungodly, nor standeth in the way of sinners, nor sitteth in the seat of the scornful.

But his delight is in the law of the Lord; and in his law doth he meditate day and night.

He shall be like a tree planted by the river of water, that bringeth forth his fruit in his season; his leaf also shall not wither; and whatsoever he doeth shall prosper.

There must be leisure and retirement, solitude and a sequestration of man's self from the noise and toil of the world; for truth scorns to be seen by eyes too much fixed upon inferior objects. — *Dr. South.*

Thou art my rock and my fortress; therefore for thy name's sake lead me and guide me.

MORNING.

INFINITE Father, before engaging in our daily duties and daily cares, we would desire to commune with our own souls, and with thee. In this morning quiet let us hear thy voice in our listening hearts. We remember that thy well-beloved Son, the sinless and perfect one, went into a mountain, apart from men, for prayer to thee. How infinite the need of such meditation and prayer for thy faltering and sinful children ! Thou hast promised to draw nigh to those who draw nigh to thee. Thou wilt reveal thy truth, and manifest thy love to the sincere and single heart. Help us to gain that singleness of heart which will prepare us to receive

so great a blessing. We need that thy Spirit should
touch our breasts to enable us to pray aright, and
truly fix our thoughts on thee. O, hear our earnest cries for the grace to make our souls meet to
become thy temple, and thy dwelling-place.

O God, our palliations for our frailties and sins
are gone when we come into thy presence. Our
vain self-defences die upon our tongues. We cannot
speak them to thine ear. We can only speak with
the confession of the publican, and plead for mercy.
And yet, O Father, though these meditations before thee prostrate us in humility, may we come to
thee in lowly joy. Set all our sins in order before
us in the light of thy countenance. May we be
strangers to all the world, rather than strangers to
our own hearts. Rend away every disguise of
selfishness and sin, and let us see what unworthy
guests we have permitted to enter into our secret
breasts, that we may drive them all away through
thy assisting grace.

And then, O God, crown all thy mercies by sending angel-thoughts to minister to us forevermore.
May we long after thee as the hart panteth after
the water-brooks. May we lay up within our souls
an unfading treasure of holy affections and heavenly
aspirations, which shall be the earnest and the foretaste of that life which is eternal. Grant us thus to
find our strength and our rest in thee, and then take
us to thyself, in that forgiving love made known by
Jesus, our Redeemer. *Amen.*

O THOU, who art the Witness and Judge of the actions and thoughts of men! We do not presume to justify ourselves in the sight of Him before whom the very heavens are not clean. If we have sinned against thee during the day which is now closing over us, we beseech thee to pardon us, and to help us by thy Holy Spirit that we sin no more.

May we be more watchful for the time to come against the wiles and snares of the world, its engrossing cares, and evil counsels, and corrupt examples. May we remember that thine eye is upon us in all places, at all times. By seasons of retirement and meditation, by reading thy holy word, by secret prayer, by holding communion with our own souls, may we nourish and strengthen this sense of the Divine Presence, and so keep ourselves from the very thought of sin.

Grant, O most merciful Father, that the experience of this day, and of all our days, may help to train us up for honor and glory and immortality, through that grace which thou hast promised in Jesus Christ, our Lord. *Amen.*

XXI.

AFFLICTION AND ADVERSITY.

Lord, shall we grumble when thy flames do scourge us ?
Our sins breathe fire ; that fire returns to purge us.
Lord, what an alchymist art thou, whose skill
Transmutes to perfect good from perfect ill.

FRANCIS QUARLES.

Call upon me in the time of trouble, so will I hear thee, and thou shalt praise me.

I will love thee, O God; being satisfied that all things, however strange and irksome they appear, shall work together for good to those that do so. — *Wilson.*

Blessed are they that mourn, for they shall be comforted.

Fortify my soul, that I may receive troubles, afflictions, disappointments, sickness, and death itself, without amazement. — *Wilson.*

Remember your comforts in the day of affliction, and your afflictions in the day of rejoicing.

If we have been bereaved of the choicest blessings, we have enjoyed them too; to be bereft is the lot of all; to enjoy is not the lot of many. — *St. Gregory of Nazianzum.*

The virtue of prosperity is temperance, the virtue of adversity is fortitude. Prosperity is the blessing of the Old Testament, adversity is the blessing of the new, which carrieth the greater benediction, and the clearer revelation of God's favor. — *Bacon.*

The disappointments I meet with may be absolutely necessary for my eternal welfare. — *Wilson.*

Let me never murmur, be dejected, or impatient, under any of the troubles of this life. — *Wilson.*

It is good that we have sometimes some troubles and crosses; for they often make a man enter into himself, and consider that he is here in banishment, and ought not to place his trust in any worldly thing. — *À Kempis.*

We have need of all our crosses. God wills our suffering, that it may purify us, and render us worthy of him. — *Fenelon.*

Through many tribulations we must enter into the kingdom of God.

Certainly virtue is like precious odors, most fragrant when they are incensed, or crushed; for prosperity doth best discover vice, but adversity doth best discover virtue. — *Anon.*

MORNING.

SUPREME Disposer! Source of all strength and consolation! Awakened by thy call from the slumbers thou hast granted, we bring our morning tribute unto thee. With lowliness of mind would we own our constant dependence on thee; and while we thank thee for what thou givest, we would be submissive in regard to whatever thou deniest, or takest from us. What have we, O Lord, that we did not receive? Why, then, should we murmur, as though something of our own was withheld from us, when thou callest us to privation?

Rather let us feel that all thou willest is best, and rejoice that, whatever affliction we may endure, thou grantest us still the light of thy countenance. May we realize that light still more, feeling, when earthly comforts depart, that thou art the all-sufficient portion of our souls; and receiving from thee that peace which the world cannot give nor take away. May we remember, when we encounter sorrow, that such has been the lot of thy faithful servants through all time; and that our blessed Saviour himself was " made perfect through sufferings." Grant us thy grace, O Lord, that, if we are called to resemble him in endurance, we may have the resemblance also of his meek submission to thee, and his earnest and loving zeal for the good of mankind. May we bear, then, steadfastly, knowing that through thy grace the hour will come when sorrow shall pass away, and those who have endured it well shall be crowned with " a far more exceeding and eternal weight of glory." Be thou with us, O Father, this day and every day; and as with us, so be thou with all who suffer, that their afflictions may be sanctified to their good; and to thee, in the blessed name of our Redeemer, be praises in the highest forever. *Amen.*

EVENING.

O THOU whose providential care is over all, whose compassion is that of a tender father or a loving mother, look upon us, thy children, as we gather around this family altar, and make our common supplications before thee. All things are subject to thy disposal, and thou doest all things well. We presume not to fathom the deep counsels of the All-wise, but where we cannot understand we would bow in perfect submission and adore. Our minds are dark, wilt thou illumine them! Our faith is weak, wilt thou strengthen it! Our thoughts wander from thee, wilt thou call them back that they may rest in thee! Our hearts are bound to the earth, wilt thou break the bonds, that our hearts may rise to thee and find in thee a perfect peace! Help us to see in all our afflictions and adversities the chastening of a father, and let us remember the gracious promises of thy holy word, and take courage ; and exchange the spirit of heaviness for that of cheerful trust, knowing that whom the Lord loveth he chasteneth, and that with every temptation he maketh a way of escape.

Sad are our memories as we recall joys that are past never to return ; but let us not forget that thou gavest what thou hast taken, and that for a season we were permitted to rejoice in the possession. If at any time the prospect seems dark before us, let us not be dismayed, but, putting our hand in thine, and following whither thou leadest, may we go on our way rejoicing, — rejoicing in thy goodness and loving-kindness, and in thy great mercy.

O God, thou wilt not forsake us, nor try us beyond our strength ; and we know thou art a very present help in time of trouble. Let us seek to learn the lesson that thou wouldst teach us, and set our affections on things above, and have our conversation in heaven, looking to Jesus, the Author and Finisher of our faith. So may we enter into his kingdom, where is fulness of joy, and dwell at thy right hand, where are pleasures evermore. *Amen.*

XXII.

SEEKING THE GLORY OF GOD.

> *Teach me, my God and King,*
> *In all things thee to see ;*
> *And what I do in anything,*
> *To do it as for thee.*
> HERBERT.

Give unto the Lord, O ye mighty, give unto the Lord glory and strength. Give unto the Lord the glory due unto his name.

Truly all human glory, all temporal honor, all worldly highness, compared to thy eternal glory is vanity and folly. — *À Kempis.*

Be thou exalted, O God, above the heavens; let thy glory be above all the earth.

We shall especially honor God, by discharging faithfully those offices which God hath intrusted us with; by improving diligently those talents which God hath committed to us. — *Dr. Barrow.*

Grant that the end of all my actions and designs may be the glory of God. — *Wilson.*

Blessed be the Lord God, the God of Israel, who only doeth wonderful things.

Blessed be his glorious name forever, and let the whole earth be filled with his glory.

Blessed be God, even the Father of our Lord Jesus Christ, the Father of mercies and the God of all comfort.

To proclaim the glory of God, to acknowledge it, to attest it in his earthly temples: this ought to be the desire of every one, the intention of all men, the end of religion. — *St. Ambrose.*

If we study to honor God, we cannot do it better than by confessing our sins, and laying ourselves low at the feet of Christ. — *Mason.*

The Lord hath prepared his throne in the heavens; and his kingdom ruleth over all.

Bless the Lord, ye his angels, that excel in strength, that do his commandments, hearkening unto the voice of his word.

Bless the Lord, all ye his hosts; ye ministers of his, that do his pleasure.

Bless the Lord, all his works in all places of his dominion: bless the Lord, O my soul.

MORNING.

ALMIGHTY God, thou hast watched over us and kept us through the night; thou hast given thy beloved sleep, and we would receive our

powers anew, refreshed by thy touch. Thy power
and wisdom and love are displayed in the wonders
of our frame, in the grateful succession of day and
night, for our labor and our rest ; in the provision
of many comforts and blessings, which thy providence hath made for us. As we arise from rest, to
enter upon the active enjoyment and use of thy
gifts, may we remember that even as it is thy glory
that thou art good, and doest good continually, so
thou art glorified by thy children, when their life is
moved by pure affections and devout trust. Help
us to seek thine honor and glory, in bringing our
souls into glad obedience to thy law and love. May
we know that to honor thee is to love thee, and to
glorify thee is to obey thee. We adore thy wonders
as they are set forth in the universe which thou hast
made. Wherever we turn, to the earth beneath, or
to the heavens above, our eyes behold the tokens of
the divine benignity and power. O God, let thy
spirit revive, and thy love satisfy our souls, till thou
shalt be exalted in our thought and glorified in our
lives. May a deep sense of being united to thee by
ties of spiritual affection give us abiding peace and
joy, that we may know what is that glory of our
God that is above the heavens.

Keep us each one to-day in thy love ; help us to
be honest, faithful, kind. And when the day is
finished, may we have the testimony of good hearts
that we have served thee, our Father and our God.
Amen.

O GOD, our Heavenly Father! May the experience of the past day help to bring us nearer to thee. At all times, and in all places, we are encompassed by the tokens of thy paternal love and care. Even the disappointments and sorrows which are mingled in our earthly lot, — help us to feel that they also are good, that they are necessary to chasten our desires, and purify our affections, and enlarge our capacities for the heavenly life.

If we can make no other return for thy unfailing goodness, may we at least show that we can be thankful. May we set thee, the Lord, always before us, remembering that our faculties are thy gift; that we are acting in thy presence; that our days are rapidly passing away; that life is a sacred trust. Whether we eat or drink, or whatsoever we do, may we do all to thy glory.

Waking or sleeping, we put our whole trust in thy mercy declared unto us by our Lord Jesus Christ. *Amen.*

XXIII.

HUMILITY.

O, learn that it is only by the lowly
  The paths of peace are trod ;
If thou wouldst keep thy garments white and holy,
  Walk humbly with thy God.

Christian Register.

I say, through the grace given unto me, to every man that is among you, not to think of himself more highly than he ought to think ; but to think soberly.

For all the world, all that we are, and all that we have, our bodies and our souls, our actions and our sufferings, our conditions at home, our accidents abroad, our many sins and our seldom virtues, are so many arguments to make our souls dwell low in the deep valleys of humility. — *Taylor.*

The humble enjoy continual peace, but in the heart of the proud is envy, and frequent indignation. — *À Kempis.*

Better it is to have a small portion of good sense with humility, and a slender understanding, than great treasures of many sciences with vain self-complacency. — *À Kempis.*

By humility and the fear of the Lord are riches and honor and life.

The truly humble Christian never inquires into the faults of his neighbor, — he takes no pleasure in judging them, — he occupies himself solely with his own. — *St. Athanasius.*

When thou canst bear grievous things, against thy will, yet willingly, know that thou hast made proficiency in humility. — *St. Ephraim.*

Every one that is proud in heart is an abomination unto the Lord : though hand join in hand, he shall not be unpunished.

God protecteth the humble and delivereth him; the humble he loveth and comforteth; unto the humble man he inclineth himself; unto the humble he giveth great grace; and after his humiliation he raiseth him to glory. — *À Kempis.*

God resisteth the proud, but giveth grace to the humble. Submit yourselves therefore to the Lord. Humble yourselves in the sight of the Lord, and he shall lift you up.

Though the Lord be high, yet hath he respect unto the lowly : but the proud he knoweth afar off.

Morning.

OUR Heavenly Father, we would draw nigh unto thee with deep humility of heart. In the light of thine infinite purity we are unholy. The sacred flame of devotion burns feebly within us. Our affections are cold and languid. We harbor wicked desires, cherish secret sins, and have transgressed thy most holy law. Weak, frail, and needy, we would seek thine almighty strength and heavenly guidance. Borne on the winds of passion, exposed to temptation, and subject to trial, we have failed to obey thee. Bow down thine ear, for we are poor and needy. We do not merit thy favor, but trust in thine infinite and constant love. Sinful as we are, thou wilt not hide thy face from us. Thine ear is open to hear the cry of thy penitent children. We rejoice that in our humiliation thou wilt hear and answer our prayers. Turn not away from the pleading of our anguished souls. Thou delightest not in sacrifice; else would we give it. The sacrifices of God are a broken spirit; a broken and a contrite heart thou wilt not despise. We come, then, in this morning hour to lay open our souls before thee. Thou knowest our inmost thoughts. Thou readest the secrets of the heart; grant us, we beseech thee, of thy renewing grace. We would walk humbly this day. May we live so near to thee, that our thoughts shall dwell in close intimacy and constant companionship with thy truth. May we so learn from the instructions and example of our Saviour as to be filled, with confidence in thy forgiving mercy, with peace and heavenly joy. May we take upon us the Christian yoke, and learn of Him who was meek and lowly of heart, and thus find rest and peace for our souls, through our Lord and Saviour Jesus Christ. *Amen.*

EVENING.

ALMIGHTY Father, Maker of heaven and earth, we indeed are, in thy sight, but as of yesterday, so imperfect is our best knowledge, so frail our own strength, and so liable are we to be overtaken with faults. But we bring before thee our tribute of praise and our supplication of prayer, because thou hast taught us, by thy Son, in all our weakness and unworthiness to come to thee, in the confidence that thou wilt not reject any who sincerely seek thy face. We would, at this hour, join our lowly homage with that which so many, as we trust, who reverence the majesty of thy great name, are offering, in the homes where thy goodness is felt. We pray that we may be more worthy of thy mercy. Show to us the needs of our own hearts. May we think of ourselves as thou dost think of us, when thou searchest us and seest our inmost thoughts. May thy goodness lead us to repentance. Wilt thou pardon the sins which we strive to forsake. May we learn of Him who gave himself for us, the just for the unjust, how to become thy true children by serving, for their good, those whom thou hast created to be with us in the world. May we seek not the honor which comes from man, but the honor which comes from God. May we trust not in ourselves, but in thy grace assisting us. And wilt thou keep us this night, and all our nights and days, from evil. *Amen.*

XXIV.

CHEERFULNESS.

Lord, with what courage and delight
I do each thing,
When thy least breath sustains my wings!
I shine and move
Like those above,
And, with much gladness
Quitting sadness,
Make me fair days of every night.

VAUGHAN.

Cheerfully perform what lieth in thee, according to the best of thy power and understanding. — *À Kempis.*

A merry heart doeth good like a medicine.

Cheerfulness and a festival spirit fills the soul full of harmony; it composes music for churches and hearts; it makes and publishes glorifications of God; it produces thankfulness and serves the end of charity. — *Taylor.*

When the oil of gladness runs over, it makes bright and tall emissions of light and holy fires, reaching up to a cloud, and making joy round about. — *Taylor.*

Therefore since it is so innocent, and may be so pious and full of holy advantage, whatsoever can innocently minister to this holy joy does set forward the work of religion and charity. — *Taylor.*

He that showeth mercy, let him do it with cheerfulness.

ɪ will be glad and rejoice in thee; I will sing praise to thy name, O thou Most High.

It is a good thing to give thanks unto the Lord, and to sing praises unto thy name, O Most High.

I will sing unto the Lord as long as I live; I will sing praise to my God while I have my being.

My meditation of him shall be sweet; I will be glad in the Lord.

If there be joy in the world, surely a man of a pure heart possesseth it. — *A Kempis.*

Let us go on our way in the simplicity of our hearts, with the peace and joy that are the fruits of the Holy Spirit. — *Fénelon.*

There is a joy which is not given to the ungodly, but to those who love Thee for thine own sake, whose joy thou thyself art. — *St. Augustine.*

Morning.

OUR Father, we thank thee for thy protection during the night that is past, and ask thy blessing on the day that is to come.

Grant us the sense of thy presence to cheer, and thy light to direct us, and give us strength for thy service. And yet more, Father, give us thine own help and blessing in our sorrows, our faintness, our failure and sin. Thou knowest that we cannot bear our burdens alone. We are only little children, and the world seems very dark to us, and our path very

hard, if we are alone. But we are thy little children ; and so we know we can come to our Father,
to ask thee to help us, and enliven us, and strength-
en us, and give us hope. We are not ashamed of
our tears, for our Lord has wept with us. We do
not ask thee to take away our sorrow, for He was
made perfect through suffering ; but we do ask thee
to be with us as thou wert with Him, our Father,
close to thy little ones, even as he as promised us.
Amen.

EVENING.

OUR Father, who art in heaven, we would close
the day at thy mercy-seat, with thy name upon
our lips, and thoughts of thee in full possession of
our hearts. Look in mercy, we beseech thee, upon
whatever in our lives to-day has not been according
to thy will ; and if we have done right, generously
serving others, in devout obedience to thee ; if we
have made evil weaker, the temptations to sin less
dangerous ; if we have made one human soul, one
of thy children, stronger, purer, better ; if we have
done aught to make light shine into dark places, and
cause Heaven to dawn upon waiting souls ; – - we
thank thee for the opportunity and power to do such
good. O that we may more and more appreciate
the privilege of being fellow-workers with thee, and
with Jesus Christ thy Son, in bringing salvation to

our fellow-men and to ourselves! Father, impress it upon us, that the true wisdom is to live and work with thee. Aid us to sound these depths. " Thou in us, and we in thee." O, give us the joy and peace of such fellowship with thy spirit, and our evenings will be peaceful, and our mornings full of hope and joy. Through all our experience thou art teaching us that there is no lasting cheerfulness, no real peace but in connection with a conscience void of offence, and an assurance that our life is near to thee, and in harmony with thy will. Gracious Father, by thy Spirit lead us to the feet of Christ. May we learn of him how to live, so that even while here below Heaven shall be open ing its bliss and glory to us.

Now we lay ourselves down to sleep, may the good angels of thy care and love be round about us. We ask for thy mercies as disciples of Jesus Christ. *Amen.*

XXV.

LOVE TO JESUS.

O Thou, at whose almighty word
  Fair light at first from darkness shone,
Teach us to know our glorious Lord,
  And trace the Father in the Son!

While we thine image, there displayed,
  With love and admiration view,
Form us in likeness to our Head,
  That we may bear thine image too.

MASON.

He that findeth Jesus, findeth a good treasure; yea, a good above all good. — *À Kempis.*

Jesus Christ, the same yesterday, and to-day, and forever.

All men should honor the Son, even as they honor the Father. He that honoreth not the Son, honoreth not the Father which hath sent him.

Jesus said, If a man love me, he will keep my words.

He that loveth me not, keepeth not my sayings: and the word which ye hear is not mine, but the Father's, which sent me.

He that hateth me, hateth my Father also.

Whosoever believeth that Jesus is the Christ, is born of God: and every one that loveth him that begat, loveth him also that is begotten of him.

Let the word of Christ dwell in you richly in all wisdom.

And whatsoever ye do in word or deed, do all in the name of the Lord Jesus, giving thanks to God and the Father by him.

Grow in grace, and in the knowledge of our Lord and Saviour Jesus Christ. To him be glory both now and forever.

MORNING.

ALMIGHTY Father, we thank thee for the manifold blessings we enjoy at thy hand. For the gift of life, — renewed this morning, — with all its opportunities and privileges; for health and the supply of our daily wants; for the ties of friendship and the sacred relation of the family circle, we thank thee.

But especially we thank thee for the gift of thy Son, our Saviour, who, by his perfect manifestation of thine infinite goodness, has revealed thee to us, as a Father we may love and trust, while we reverence and adore.

May the gratitude which should fill our hearts overflow in affection for him who has rendered us this inestimable service; and may that affection bring forth fruits worthy of its divine prompting. May it make us patient and forbearing, cheerful, unselfish, trustful. Bring us nearer to thee. Help us to feel that this blessed Saviour was sent to draw us closer to thine embrace, — even us, of this family group: and while we acknowledge our unfitness, our shortcomings and imperfections, may the remembrance of his pure life — though he was tempted in all points as we are — stimulate us to walk in the narrow path which leadeth upwards to thy throne.

Teach us to know Christ, — which knowledge is sufficient, with thy blessing, to make us wise unto salvation, — salvation from sin, and the suffering of a guilty conscience.

Our petitions we offer in the name of thy Son, our Saviour. *Amen.*

EVENING.

O GOD, in whom we live, so great and so infinitely above us, and yet so near, — filling immensity with thy presence, and yet dwelling closely with the lowliest of thy creatures; adorable in thy majesty and power, and yet so tender and worthy to be loved, — we would draw near to thee in humble and grateful praise.

It is Thou that givest to all things their being. Thou givest to the stars their light, and to the earth its fruits, and to each one of us the blessings of our lives.

And yet, O our Father, how forgetful we have been of thee! Forgive us, Almighty God. And now, as we resign ourselves again to thy watchful care, help us to realize thy goodness, and return to thee love for love.

Above all, we remember Him whom thou didst send into the world, as pledge and manifestation of the infinite richness of thy grace. Gratefully and tremblingly we thank thee for this precious gift, and for the assurance, that, in the mildness and compassion of Jesus, and in his tender, unwearied love, we see only the reflection of thyself.

O, let it not be that he has come to us in vain! May the remembrance of his holy life, and of his love for man, of his prayers for our redemption, his acts of goodness and his death for our sake, melt and conquer our forgetful and rebellious hearts. And may our narrow and sensual natures expand with a purer affection, as we behold the glory of God in the face of Jesus Christ.

Teach us, through loving him, to imitate his spirit. May we become pure, as he was pure, and, like him, may we make it our meat and drink to do thy holy will.

And unto thee, through him, we would render glory and praise, now and evermore. *Amen.*

5 *

XXVI.

AGAINST ANGER.

Quench Thou the fires of hate and strife,
The wasting fever of the heart;
From perils guard our feeble life,
And to our souls thy peace impart.
BREVIARY.

Be not hasty in thy spirit to be angry, for anger resteth in the bosom of fools.

First keep thyself in peace, and then shalt thou be able to pacify others. — *À Kempis.*

He that is slow to anger is better than the mighty ; and he that ruleth his spirit, than he that taketh a city.

A passionate man turneth even good to evil, and easily believeth the worst. — *À Kempis.*

Anger, of all passions, endeavors most to make reason useless. It is neither manly nor ingenuous. It is a confluence of all the irregular passions : there is in it envy and sorrow, fear and scorn, pride and prejudice, rashness and inconsideration, rejoicing in evil and a desire to inflict it, self love, impatience, and curiosity. — *Taylor.*

Give me a mild and meek and peaceable spirit, that, remembering my own infirmities, I may bear with those of others. — *Wilson.*

The fruit of the Spirit is love, joy, peace, long-suffering, gentleness, goodness, faith, meekness, temperance.

An angry man stirreth up strife, and a furious man aboundeth in transgression.

Let all bitterness, and wrath, and anger, and clamor, and evil speaking, be put away from you, with all malice.

Cease from anger, and forsake wrath; fret not thyself in any wise to do evil.

He that is slow to wrath is of great understanding; but he that is hasty of spirit exalteth folly.

Morning.

O THOU Eternal One, whose power created and whose presence guides all thy works, we praise thee with grateful hearts that we are considered worthy of existence in thy creation! We thank thee that we, who are so weak amid powers so awful, who are so helpless in the midst of necessities so pressing, so liable to sin where the effects of sin are so cruel, can look up to thee, the Creator and Ruler of all, and feel that our poor souls are more precious in thy sight than all the universe beside; that, with all thy cares, thou dost still care for us; with all thy working in *law*, thou dost still bless and help and inspire, in the liberty of love. As we find ourselves driven about by destinies which we cannot control, and see our fondest hopes perish, and our most cherished interests fail, help us, O our Father, to feel that all things are ordered in love; that our disappointments are our best discipline, and our failures the occasions of our best and truest success. May we, therefore, not faint when we are rebuked of thee, knowing that thou dost not chasten us for thy pleasure, but for our profit.

Save us from all impatience and restiveness under the discipline of our lot. Especially save us from anger. Help us to restrain the fearful passion ere it rise in harsh words, or frowning looks, or cruel deeds; ere it destroy our peace of mind and the happiness of all with whom we are associated. Thou knowest the bitterness of our repentance, whenever we yield to this enemy of all that is beautiful and blessed in life; how we loathe our weakness and folly! Save us, we pray thee, from the unrest and wretchedness which follow all transgressions. May we overcome the evil within us, by loving all that is good and lovely in others, and, by helping our neighbor, forget, and thus conquer ourselves. Hear us in this earnest prayer of our hearts. Keep us this day in purity and peace, and may we do, think, feel, nothing which is not acceptable in thy sight; and to thy name shall be the glory and honor forever. *Amen.*

EVENING.

HOLY and good God, our Father, we thank thee for life through another day. Thou

hast given us strength to bear its burdens and perform its duties. Through thee we have enjoyed its
good and escaped its dangers. Thy power is over
us, a covering and a defence by night. Day and
night are thine, and for both we praise and give
thee thanks, who alone makest us to dwell in safety.
For whatsoever of good we have had strength and
opportunity to do, we give thee the glory, for it is
thou who workest in us both to will and to do of
thy good pleasure. With the labors and cares of
the day that is gone, help us to lay aside all evil
and unhappy feelings, and to be at rest. May
there be in us no discontent with thy Providence,
no impatience or ill will towards our fellow-beings.
Now, in the stillness of the night, we call thee to
mind, whom too often we forget in the noise of the
day. We rejoice that thou art ever mindful of us.
If this day we have knowingly sinned against thee,
may we sincerely repent, and make confession in
our hearts to thee ; and do thou, O God, forgive
us, and make our repentance effectual. How rich
thy love, which has blessed us so long and abundantly ! When we have turned from thee, and
done wrong, and in many things come short of our
duty, thou hast not in anger cast us off, but hast
still been kind. May thy tender mercy to us lead
us to be patient and kind to each other and to all.
May we live in love, that thou mayest dwell in us.
Let us not suffer any angry or resentful thought to

remain in us now, a spring of sin and bitterness, driving out thy Holy Spirit. May we truly and wholly forgive any that have injured or caused pain to us. We ask of thee the sleep which renews our weary bodies, but first we pray that thy peace may be in our hearts, that we may lie down in charity with all.

God of our lives and Father of our spirits, watch over us, and those whom we love; keep us from danger, suffering, and death. Yet prepare us, O God, for the night from which we shall not wake on earth, that we may rise from it to an eternal and blessed life.

Grant us thy blessing, through Jesus, our Lord and Saviour, in whom we praise and glorify thee, our Father and God. *Amen.*

XXVII.

WEARY NOT IN WELL-DOING.

O, may I never faint nor tire,
　　Nor, wandering, leave His sacred ways!
Great God! accept my soul's desire,
　　And give me strength to live thy praise.

MRS. STEELE.

Be not wearied out by the labors which thou hast undertaken for my sake, nor let tribulations cast thee down ever at all; but let my promise strengthen and comfort thee under every circumstance. — *À Kempis.*

The labor of the righteous tendeth to life; the fruit of the wicked, to sin.

A faithful man shall abound with blessings.

Let us not be weary in well-doing, for in due season we shall reap if we faint not.

Happy that soul which death finds rich, not in gold, furniture, learning, reputation, or barren purposes and desires, but in good works. — *Wilson.*

For God is not unrighteous to forget your work and labor of love, which ye showed towards his name.

Be not slothful, but followers of them who, through faith and patience, inherit the promises.

For religion cannot change, though we do; and, if we do, we have left God; and whither he can go that goes from God, his own sorrows will soon enough instruct him. — *Taylor.*

The Lord giveth power to the faint; and to them that have no might he increaseth strength.

They that wait on the Lord shall renew their strength.

They shall mount up with wings, as eagles; they shall run, and not be weary; and they shall walk, and not faint.

To him that overcometh will I grant to sit with me in my throne, even as I also overcame, and am set down with my Father in his throne.

MORNING.

WE thank thee, O thou Preserver of men, that thou hast permitted us to wake, refreshed

by the repose of the night, to behold the cheering
light of the morning, and to enter with renewed
strength upon the duties of another day.   We
adore thee for thy unwearied mercy, of which we
have been constantly partakers. We bless thee
that thou hast given us intelligence to perceive, and
hearts to feel, thy ever-flowing goodness. With
our minds and our hearts would we praise thee.   O
that we might also glorify thee, this day, in our
lives! Quicken us, we beseech thee, to do thy will.
Let gratitude incite us to diligence in thy service.
Let thy new blessings provoke us to new obedience.
Help us, O Lord, to resume, this day, the great
work of life with renewed zeal and resolution.   If
it be thy will, may it be a day of activity and accom-
plishment.   May we do with our might whatsoever
our hands find to do.   May we not yield to sloth or
any weakness.   May each hour be well spent, and
each duty, as it presents itself, be met with a cheerful and devoted spirit, — be done as for thee, with
the alacrity of filial love.

We pray for courage, fortitude, and persever-
ance.   Strengthen us, O Lord, with might by thy
Spirit in the inner man.   Let our hearts be set to
do one thing, — to reach forth towards what is before; to press towards the mark for the prize of the
high calling of God in Christ Jesus, our Lord; —
turning neither to the right hand nor to the left
from the narrow way that leadeth unto life.   O

that we might be able to spend this day in such a manner as to approve ourselves in thy sight; to keep a conscience void of offence; to perform useful service to our fellow-men, and lay up for ourselves treasure in heaven, — so that if, in thy wise providence, it should be the last of our earthly days, it may be the best and brightest!

But, Heavenly Father, whatever the day may bring forth, — whether strength or weakness, joy or sorrow, success or failure, life or death, be awaiting us in its unknown course, — we would go forward without anxiety or apprehension; trusting all to thee, to whom we breathe our prayer, and who wilt cause all things to work together for good to them that seek thee. Hallowed be thy name. Thy kingdom come; thy will be done on earth, as it is in heaven. Give us this day our daily bread. Forgive us our debts, as we forgive our debtors. And lead us not into temptation; but deliver us from evil; for thine is the kingdom, and the power, and the glory, forever. *Amen.*

EVENING.

O BLESSED God, the day is thine, the night also is thine. Thine infinite patience and love are still over us, and, as we lie down to rest, we would feel a reverent confidence and joy that thou art our keeper. The day that has closed has

H

carried its record up to thee. Forgive us, O God, if in anything we have been unfaithful or unkind. Let us contemplate thy goodness and faithfulness until we shall feel the joy of a soul filled with duty and love. Thou knowest our weakness, how our good purposes and pure desires too often weary and faint. We need thine aid. O condemn us not, but pity us and help us according to thy love. If we have failed of any good intent which we felt in our hearts when we went out in the morning, O renew our mind, that, if our lives are preserved, we may return to our duty on the morrow with stronger and holier purpose; may we be supported by the thought that, whatever we do as unto God, is a service of God which thou wilt not despise. And so may our common labors continually refresh our souls with the consciousness of thine approval. Keep us to-night; give us sweet sleep, and awake us in the morning to joy and gladness in thee. *Amen.*

XXVIII.

SOWING AND REAPING.

Do thy best always, — do it now, —
For in the present time,
As in the furrows of a plough,
Fall seeds of good or crime.

The sun and rain will ripen fast
Each seed that thou hast sown ;
And every act and word at last
By its own fruit be known.

JONES VERY.

They that sow in tears shall reap in joy.

He that goeth forth and weepeth, bearing precious seed, shall doubtless come again with rejoicing, bringing his sheaves with him.

Blessed are ye that sow beside all waters.

He that soweth sparingly, shall reap sparingly ; and he that soweth bountifully, shall reap bountifully.

They that plough iniquity, and sow wickedness, reap the same.

Sow to yourselves in righteousness, reap in mercy ; break up the fallow ground ; for it is time to seek the Lord, till he come and rain righteousness upon you.

Ye have ploughed wickedness, ye have reaped iniquity.

Be not deceived : God is not mocked ; for whatsoever a man soweth, that shall he also reap.

For he that soweth to his flesh, shall of the flesh reap corruption ; but he that soweth to the spirit, shall of the spirit reap life everlasting.

He that soweth iniquity shall reap vanity.

The wicked worketh a deceitful work : but to him that soweth righteousness shall be a sure reward.

Now he that ministereth seed to the sower, both minister bread for your food, and multiply your seed sown, and increase the fruits of your righteousness.

Being enriched in everything to all bountifulness, which causeth through us thanksgiving to God.

MORNING.

WITH the new day, we would again offer before the Most High God our gratitude and praise. By thy good Spirit are the minds and hearts of thy people taught, and guided, and sanctified. By thy holy Providence are every good word and work encouraged. And we pray that thy blessing may rest upon the efforts of thy children to promote the cause of truth and right in all the world. May thy wisdom fill the souls of those who teach. May success attend those who attempt the relief of sorrow and suffering. We desire to be in true sympathy with all who seek to build up thy kingdom on earth, and to join with them in labors and sacrifices, as we have fit opportunity.

Strengthen the hands and establish the hearts of

such as anywhere bear testimony to the Gospel of thy Son. Bless thy servant, our pastor, and those who are helping his work. Bless the church and society with which we are connected. Build it up in the most holy faith. Let no discouragement hinder the fidelity of the members to their duty. Amid all changes, may we feel that the good seed of thy word is not sown in vain. May the fruits of thy salvation abound. May the young remember thee in the morning of their days, and the aged be filled with thy peace, and all to whom thou givest strength do thy work till thy kingdom shall fully come. This, and all our prayers, we would offer in the name of our Lord and Saviour Jesus Christ. *Amen.*

EVENING.

O GOD, our ever-present Friend and Father, thy providence has watched over us and blessed us through another day. We have been made glad by new gifts from thee. Thou hast bestowed new means of progress in knowledge and in purity, new opportunities of service to thee and to our fellow-men. We confess our sinful neglects, our inexcusable misimprovement of the talents committed to our trust. We mourn that we have failed to listen to so many of the angels of thy love, whom thou hast graciously sent to call us to works of truth and love. But, O Father, if we have been moved to do anything this day, or in former days, in accordance with thy will, we give unto thee the glory and the praise.

Father, help us to realize the responsibility that rests upon us. Save us from sowing the seeds of evil in our hearts, or in the world, by our unfaithfulness or our sin. Aid us, day by day, to plant that love and patience and purity within our own souls and in others' breasts, which shall bring forth blessed fruits, an hundred-fold. Thou wilt not deliver us from the just retribution for our misdeeds, but thou wilt open all the treasures of thy grace to crown the efforts of every true and loving heart.

Father, we thank thee that thou dost permit us to become ministers of good to other souls. Even such as we may do something to carry forward thy purposes of mercy, for thou dost accept the smallest service of faith and love, and bestow upon it thy benediction. Deliver us from the pride that buries any single talent in the earth, because we have not been endowed with greater gifts. May we not despise the lowly work which seems great in thy sight. May we rejoice to send one new ray of light into darkened homes ; to excite one new pulse of joy in the sorrowing breast. May we thus learn to go about doing good, remembering that every smallest ministry to the least of these his brethren is a ministry to him who is our Master and Lord.

O God, we can only work in faith and trust, but we know that thou wilt permit no seed of holy effort to be sown in vain. When the day of life shall close, O grant that we may be found to have been faithful to life's solemn trusts, and fitted to receive the benediction, " Enter into the joy of your Lord." Hear our prayer, for thy infinite mercy's sake. *Amen.*

XXIX. ·

FIDELITY IN DAILY DUTIES.

All may of thee partake ;
Nothing so small can be,
But draws, when acted for thy sake,
Greatness and worth from thee.

If done beneath thy laws,
Even servile labors shine ;
Hallowed is toil, if this the cause,
The meanest work divine.

HERBERT.

A man's virtue is not to be measured by his great attempts, but by his common actions. — *Pascal.*

He that is faithful in that which is least, is faithful also in much ; and he that is unjust in the least, is unjust also in much.

The desire of the slothful killeth him ; for his hands refuse to labor.

He coveteth greedily all the day long; but the righteous giveth and spareth not.

In the morning sow thy seed, and in the evening withhold not thine hand.

See that ye walk circumspectly, not as fools, but as wise; redeeming the time, because the days are evil.

And whatsoever ye do, in word or deed, do all in the name of the Lord Jesus, giving thanks to God and the Father by him.

It is only by fidelity in little things that a true and constant love to God can be distinguished from a passing fervor of spirit. — *Fénelon.*

It is with piety as with the mysterious ladder that was exhibited to the patriarch Jacob, the foot of which rested on the earth, but the summit reached the skies; it is only by degrees that we can ascend, but it is by degrees that we can finally arrive at the highest elevation of which our nature is capable. — *St. Basil.*

Observed duties maintain our credit, but secret duties maintain our life. — *Flavel.*

Morning.

OUR Heavenly Father, we come with the light of thy morning about us, and with the dawn of hope and aspiration within us, to praise and glorify thee, from whom are all light and strength. We come, O Father, trusting in thy tender mercy and loving-kindness that thou wilt forgive all our transgressions, wilt strengthen the better purposes of our hearts, and wilt shine upon our souls with continually brighter radiance, until thou shalt bring us unto the endless day in which they dwell who perfectly do thy will.

We thank thee that we are permitted again to take our place among the great company of thy servants who wait, on earth and in heaven, to perform thy bidding ; and *we*, too, would wait with humble, trustful hearts, looking to thee alone for the power to do the work which this day shall put into our hands. Grant, we beseech thee, that these hours may be marked by faithfulness in all the duties that thou layest upon us, in the spirit, not of fear, but of love. Teach us that there is nothing small and nothing great before thee, but that thou art as well pleased with the scanty service which we can offer thee in the common occupations of our daily lives, as with the greatest deeds of saints and martyrs, being satisfied if we have done what we could. Strengthen us against temptation, and confirm us in the feeling of our constant dependence upon thee. Help us to overcome the tumultuous strife within, and the enticements from without us, which would distract our thoughts from thee, and to recognize, in everything which thou givest us to do, thy hand in wisdom leading us on and disciplining us, by the small requirements and petty cares of this earthly life, for the grander opportunities of service which, in thy eternal world, shall be given

to those who here have listened to the voice of
duty and have not been disobedient to the heavenly
vision.

Hear and accept our petitions, we pray thee, in
the name of Jesus Christ our Lord. *Amen.*

EVENING.

ALMIGHTY God, we have always to thank
thee for thy kindness, — and again we close
the day with our grateful prayer. The events of
each day reveal anew thy love and care for us. Do
not let us trust in our own wisdom or our own
strength, but teach us thy way, and make us rest
on thy right arm. Show us what we can do each
day, that thy kingdom may more quickly come; and
with thy Spirit inspire our spirits, that we may do it
bravely and cheerfully, as thy children. May the
devotions of this hour help to prepare us for to-
morrow's duty, help us to stand firmly and labor
faithfully.

Bless us with thy watchful care as we retire to
rest, and may our sleep be peaceful and refreshing.
We know that thou wilt hear our prayer, because
thou hast promised in thy Son that thou wilt give
thy little flock the victory. We come to thee in
his name. *Amen.*

XXX.

THE LOVE OF GOD.

O Source divine, and Life of all,
The Fount of being's wondrous sea !
Thy depth would every heart appall,
That saw not Love supreme in thee.

STERLING.

We have known and believed the love that God hath to us. God is love.

Herein is love, not that we loved God, but that he loved us.

How excellent is thy loving-kindness, O God! therefore the children of men put their trust under the shadow of thy wings.

In this was manifested the love of God towards us, because that God sent his only begotten Son into the world, that we might live through him.

For I am persuaded, that neither death, nor life, nor angels, nor principalities, nor powers, nor things present, nor things to come,

Nor height, nor depth, nor any other creature, shall be able to separate us from the love of God which is in Christ Jesus our Lord.

If God be for us, who can be against us ?

Blessed be the God and Father of our Lord Jesus Christ, who hath blessed us with all spiritual blessings.

The eyes of the Lord are over the righteous, and his ears

are open unto their prayers ; but the face of the Lord is against them that do evil.

Good and upright is the Lord, therefore will he teach sinners in the way.

The Lord is good unto them that wait for him, to the soul that seeketh him.

The love of men is good, whilst it lasteth ; the love of God is better, being *everlasting.* — *Warwick.*

MORNING.

IN the light of this new day, thou Father of lights and of mercies, we rejoice to behold a new token of thy goodness. While day unto day uttereth speech, may our ears be open to hear, and our hearts to welcome, the glad tidings which heaven and earth are telling of thee. May we learn to see thee in all thy works, and, amid the bountiful gifts of thy Providence, feel more the kindness reaching down to us than the gift which it bestows. May all that is bright and beautiful around us speak to us of thy transcendent goodness, thine unchanging love. May all that is endearing in our friends remind us of a friendship more dear and sacred. Through things seen and temporal may we learn to behold the riches and the glory of thine unseen and eternal kingdom. By the daily consecration of ourselves to thee, by prayer, by devout and holy living, may we experience in our hearts the exceeding richness of thy grace and the tenderness of thy love. May we live on earth lives of thankfulness and praise, and having, each day, finished the work which thou hast given us to do, may we enter into the rest which remaineth for the people of God, through thy great mercy in Jesus Christ our Lord. *Amen.*

EVENING.

WE bless thee, O God, for all thy gifts, but most of all for the gift of thyself. We ask for thine help, that we may receive all familiar blessings as from thy bountiful hand ; but yet more fervently do we pray that in them we may receive thee, and by them be made to live and move and have our being in thy love.

May we thus take our daily bread from thee, and find in it the food alike of the soul and of the body, knowing that we are not to live by bread alone, but by every word from the mouth of God. On thy living and eternal word may we day by day be fed, and do thou graciously give us evermore this heavenly bread. In the things that thou hast made may we seek and enjoy thee, the Maker. May the light be to us the brightness of thy glory, the air the breath of thy spirit, the water the fountain of thy truth, and the worlds the work of thy power.

We bless thee for the gift of love, and for the

crown of this gift, the faculty of knowing and loving thee. We rejoice that thou hast condescended to draw near to us, thy dependent, waiting creatures, and as the known God, the Father in heaven, to visit us with grace, and to ask to abide with us in thy comforting Spirit. Thou art more ready to bless us than we are to ask thy blessing, and what thy work and thy providence have always signified, thy gospel fully declares, — that thou wouldest give thyself to us, the children of men, and make us the children of God.

All glory be to thee, the Heavenly Father, for him in whom thy love dwelt and dwells in such unspeakable fulness, Jesus Christ, thy Son, our Saviour. May we love thee in him, and him in thee. Give us, O give us, through him and by thy Spirit, a blessed sense of oneness with thy family on earth and in heaven, that, no longer broken branches, we may abide in the true vine, and, no longer lost sheep, we may be of the one fold and the one Shepherd.

Hear us in this our lowly prayer, through Jesus Christ our Lord. *Amen.*

XXXI.

DEAL JUSTLY, AND LOVE MERCY.

O, blest the man whose aims and ardors rise
On Faith's strong pinions soaring to the skies ;
Yet, while conversing here with want and woe,
Acts the good minister of Heaven below.
The poor relieved, the widow's wrongs redressed,
The darkened mind illumed with heavenly day,
The sympathies, that soothe the burdened breast
*   And wipe Affliction's tear away, —*
*   These on the friendly, generous mind*
*   Will draw God's choicest blessings down ;*
*   He'll mercy show for mercies shown,*
*   And still be kindest to the kind.*
HENRY MOORE.

Thus speaketh the Lord of hosts, saying, Execute true judgment, and show mercy and compassion every man to his brother :

And oppress not the widow nor the fatherless, the stranger nor the poor.

Have we not all one father ? hath not our God created us ? why do we deal treacherously every man against his brother ?

Render to all their dues.

The wicked borroweth, and payeth not again ; but the righteous showeth mercy, and giveth.

He is ever merciful, and lendeth ; and his seed is blessed.

Defend the poor and fatherless ; do justice to the afflicted and needy.

Let no man put a stumbling-block, or an occasion to fall, in his brother's way.

A good man showeth favor, and lendeth : he will guide his affairs with discretion.

Withhold not good from them to whom it is due, when it is in the power of thine hand to do it.

The merciful man doeth good to his own soul; but he that is cruel troubleth his own flesh.

Woe unto him that buildeth his house by unrighteousness, and his chambers by wrong.

He that hath pity upon the poor lendeth unto the Lord; and that which he hath given will he pay him again.

He that by usury and unjust gain increaseth his substance, he shall gather it for him that will pity the poor.

MORNING.

O THOU infinite Parent, who by thy providence dost enrich us every day with innumerable blessings, we thank thee for thy goodness. As we remember thy mercies, may there spring up in our hearts the feeling of universal kindness, and may our lives be so pervaded with the religion of thy Son, that, like him, we may go about doing good. We would now lift up our affections in ardent prayer. Kindle within us a devout fervor of soul. On the wings of faith may our thoughts rise heavenward. But while thus we would cherish devout sentiments, grant that we also may go forth to the duties of this day with the love of our fellow-men dwelling within us. May we be kind and charitable in our judgments, loving mercy, dealing justly, and walking humbly before thee. Strengthen within us the desire to relieve the needy, to lift up the downcast and degraded, and to do something to diminish the wickedness and woe of the world. We pray for men in all conditions of outward life and inward states of mind. We would carry on our hearts to thee the memory of the slave. May the days of his bondage be numbered, and cause the light of universal liberty to be rapidly spread abroad. Hasten the day when thy glorious kingdom shall come and thy will be done on earth as in heaven. May we thy children walk in the footsteps of our Master and do all in our power to wipe away the tear of sorrow and soothe the heart in its anguish; and, by our ready and tender sympathy, encourage the weak, cheer the desponding, enlighten the ignorant, and reform the sinful. Increase our faith in the power of true religion as a means of the world's redemption, and through the benign and healing influences of the Gospel may there come the reign of happiness, virtue, and peace. With lowly self-denial, may we so live every day as to help bear others' burdens, and give proof of our love of thee, whom we have not seen, by our love of our brother, whom we have seen; and thus, by fidelity to the

6 *

great law of love, have our souls created anew in
Christ.   May we in heart and life be formed in the
Saviour's image, through whom to thee would we
render eternal praise and thanksgiving, world without end.   *Amen.*

EVENING.

ALMIGHTY and most merciful God, we acknowledge thy goodness in permitting us to
enjoy another day, filled with the manifestations of
thy loving care.

Give to us more and more of that faith which
works by love and overcomes the world.   May we
show that we are Christians, by the care with which
we fulfil every sacred trust; by meekness and gentleness and long-suffering in all our domestic relations; by keeping our thoughts and affections pure;
by sympathizing in each other's troubles, and bearing each other's burdens, — doing justly, loving
mercy, and walking humbly with God.

O Thou in whose hands our breath is, and whose
are all our ways! we do not trust in ourselves; we
trust in thee.   So long as we continue in this world
of difficulty and trial, take not thine holy Spirit
from us, but lift upon us the light of thy countenance, and give us peace; and, at the last, receive
us unto thyself, through thine infinite mercy in Him
who loved us and gave himself for us.   *Amen.*

XXXII.

LIFE EVERLASTING.

Forever blessed they,
    Whose joyful feet shall stand,
While endless ages waste away,
    Amid that glorious band.

My soul would thither tend,
    While toilsome years are given;
Then let me, gracious God, ascend
    To sweet repose in heaven.

R. PALMER.

There is one life, — to look forward to the life above. There is one death, — sin; for it is that which destroys the soul. — *St. Gregory.*

What shall I do, that I may inherit eternal life?

Thou shalt love the Lord thy God with all thy heart, and with all thy soul, and with all thy mind; and thou shalt love thy neighbor as thyself.

Verily I say unto you, There is no man that hath left house, or parents, or brethren, or wife, or children, for the kingdom of God's sake, who shall not receive manifold more in this present time, and in the world to come life everlasting.

Write, read, chant, mourn, keep silence, pray, endure crosses manfully: life everlasting is worth all these conflicts, and greater than these. — *À Kempis.*

These things have I written unto you that believe on the name of the Son of God; that ye may know that ye have eternal life, and that ye may believe on the name of the Son of God.

Verily, verily, I say unto you, he that believeth on me hath everlasting life.

Make now friends to thyself by honoring the saints of God, and imitating their actions, that when thou failest in this short life, they may receive thee into everlasting habitations. — À *Kempis.*

God will render to every man according to his deeds: to them who, by patient continuance in well-doing, seek for glory, and honor, and immortality, eternal life.

Eternal life, which God, that cannot lie, promised before the world began.

Morning.

ETERNAL and ever-merciful God, our heavenly Father, thou art the father of light and the source of blessedness. Day unto day uttereth speech of thee. Each new morning calls on us to praise thee and give thanks for thy goodness. We commit ourselves to thee, to be guided, upheld, and saved by thee this day. Lead us, O our Father, in thy way, though it be a way we have not known, and we will rejoice and trust in thee, assured that no evil will befall us while thou art our guardian and guide. Let no sin have dominion over us, to bring guilt and sorrow into our hearts. O thou God and Father of our Lord Jesus Christ, we praise thee that through him thou hast brought life and immortality to light, and hast begotten us again by his resurrection from the dead to an inheritance incorruptible, undefiled, and that fadeth not away.

May we have that unfeigned faith in him by which we shall pass from death unto life. He is our way and thy truth; and by our hearty belief that thou didst send him into the world, may he become the life of our souls. Suffer us not to hold the truth in unrighteousness; knowing that our Lord, who once died for sin, now liveth in heaven, may we die to sin that we may live to him and to thee. By patient continuance in well-doing may we seek for honor, glory, and immortality, and finally attain to everlasting life. May Christ be formed in us the hope of glory. May our affections be set on things above, and our life be hid with Christ in God.

We rejoice, O God, in the works of thy hands. May we ever see thee in nature. May we also know thee in the testimony of our own consciences, so that in the knowledge of thee, and of Jesus, whom thou didst send, we may have eternal life.

Help us by thy grace this day to honor thee in keeping thy commandments. May we not love thee in word alone, but in deed and in truth, and so may we love each other and all around us, seeking not our own, but each the other's good. Bless and keep our friends. Let thy favor be upon our land, and thy truth come to all nations. Forgive us our sins, and help us to forsake them. May we also forgive, as we hope to be forgiven. And unto Him who loved us, and gave himself for us, and through Him to thee, be glory, honor, and dominion ascribed now and evermore. *Amen.*

EVENING.

O GOD, Fountain of all life, we thank thee for thy good gift of the waters of life through another day. We bless thee that we live and move and have our being *in* thee. The world presses hard upon us, and we might faint and die if we were alone; but we are not alone, for the Father is with us. Not one moment in all our life is passed without thee; thou wilt never leave us. No place is without thee; thou wilt never forsake us. Thou hast made us for life, thou hast kept us in life. When our last night in this world shall close about us, thy love will fold us to sleep, and when we awake in the life to come, we shall be still with thee, for in thy love we shall live forever. Our sun shall be turned into darkness, this earth shall pass away from our sight, the body shall return to the dust as it was, but the Sun that lights the sun shall shine forever. The hand in which the earth is but a speck of dust abides. Thou art the same; thy years shall not fail; and we are the sons of God. Not our will, but thy will made us; not our will, but thine, has kept us this day. O God, our Father, help us to a deeper trust in the life everlasting, from the lesson of this one day. May we *feel* that this love which is now ever shall be; this robe of the flesh is thy gift to thy child, and when it is worn out thou wilt clothe him again; this work of life is the work thou hast given us to do, and when it is done thou wilt give us more; this love, that makes all our life so glad, flows out of the deep fountain of God, for God is love, and we shall love forever. O, set these lessons deep in our hearts; help us to feel how, day by day, we see some dim shadow of the eternal day that will break upon us at the last. May the Gospel of thy Son, the whisper of thy Spirit, unite to make our faith in the life to come solid and clear; then shall we be glad when thou shalt call us, and enter into thy glory in Jesus Christ. *Amen.*

XXXIII.

DWELL THOU WITH US.

O, make our house Thy sanctuary !
Come in to us, a friendly guest,
And in our circle ever tarry ;
Then shall we be forever blest,
And thou, an inmate of these walls,
Transfigure them to royal halls.

REV. C. T. BROOKS, from the German.

The Most High dwelleth not in temples made with hands; as saith the prophet, Heaven is my throne, and earth is my footstool : what house will ye build me ? saith the Lord; or what is the place of my rest ?

Ye are the temple of the living God; as God hath said, I will dwell in them, and walk in them; and I will be their God, and they shall be my people.

But will God, in very deed, dwell with men upon the earth ? Behold heaven, and the heaven of heavens cannot contain thee !

Jesus said, If a man love me, he will keep my words : and my Father will love him, and we will come unto him, and make our abode with him.

Narrow is the mansion of my soul : enlarge thou it, that thou mayest enter in. It is ruinous, repair thou it; it has that within which must offend thine eye ; but who shall cleanse it ? or to whom should I cry, save thee ? — *St. Augustine.*

If ye love me, keep my commandments.

And I will pray the Father, and he shall give you another Comforter, that he may abide with you forever.

And this is his commandment : that we should believe on the name of his Son Jesus Christ, and love one another.

And he that keepeth his commandments dwelleth in him, and he in him.

And hereby we know that he abideth in us, by the Spirit which he hath given us.

Morning.

OUR Father who art in heaven, and who art not far from any one of us, thy children on earth, when we awake we are still with thee. Help us draw nigh unto thee in the spirit, that we may feel how near thou always art unto us. Teach us that the heaven where thou lovest to dwell is in the heart and in the home of the pure and the lowly. Open thou our eyes that we may see this place to be none other but the house of God, and its lowly door the gate of heaven. Open our hearts by the gentle urgencies of thy Spirit, that thy Christ and all thy holy angels may come in and abide with us as welcome guests. Thou who hast been our dwelling-place in all generations, O dwell thou with us and within us to-day.

Once more the light of the visible heaven, which declares thy handiwork, shines in through the windows of our earthly tabernacle to guide and to gladden our daily toil. O, let the light of thy spiritual presence, as imaged in the face of Jesus Christ, in like manner shine in upon our souls to quicken our affections and to guide our thoughts to thee. May this new morning kindle in us a new desire to live as children of the day. May we walk and work as seeing Him who is invisible. May we see and share thy endless and boundless activity of beneficence, entering into the joy of our Lord. Let thy works appear unto thy servants, and thy glory unto their children, and let the beauty of the Lord our God be upon us. Guide us this day and all our days with thy counsel, and afterward receive us to glory. *Amen.*

EVENING.

GOD of the evening, while its shades deepen around us, we come to thee. We give thee thanks for what the day has bestowed: for protection, for sustenance, for the blessings that have crowned us ; yes, even for the trials that have been sent to bring us nearer to thyself. " The day is thine," and through the day thou hast been with us. " The night also is thine "; through night be near us still. Be near, not only as thou art, in thine infinity, present everywhere, but as thou art with thy people, looking on them with approval, and granting them the sweet assurance of thy love. Thou hast said that thy dwelling is with the lowly and with him of contrite heart ; thus in lowliness and penitence for sin, enable us to seek thee and to find thee near.

Abide with us, O Lord, " for the day is far spent." Abide to defend our dwelling from outward evil, and to guard our hearts from every unworthy thought and feeling. Be thy protection not with us alone, but with the traveller on the land or on the deep, the soldier in his tent, the captive in his cell. Be with those in sorrow and those in gladness, with those in the fulness of strength and those drawing near to death. As thou sendest to the wearied children of men thy freshening gift of sleep, send to the souls of all spiritual refreshment, that good purposes may be formed or strengthened anew, for patient endurance or for active duty.

Abide with us, for the day of life is drawing — how nearly we know not! — toward its close. Be with us, ever that we may be prepared; be with us when that close shall come; and then may we go to our final rest with calmness, even as now to our slumber, knowing that thou art with us still. Grant unto us thine approving presence, not in time alone, but in eternity; and, awaking in the light of heaven, may we be ever with the Lord. To thee, in the name of Him who is one with thee, and through whom we have access to thy throne, be praises evermore. *Amen.*

XXXIV.

A SUSTAINING HOPE.

Hope humbly, then; with trembling pinions soar,
Wait the great teacher, Death, and God adore;
What uture bliss, he gives not thee to know,
But gives that hope to be thy blessing now.
POPE.

Happy is he that hath the God of Jacob for his help, whose hope is in the Lord his God.

Hope is like the wing of an angel soaring up to heaven, and bears our prayers to the throne of God. — *Taylor.*

The hope of the righteous shall be gladness, but the expectation of the wicked shall perish.

Without hope it is impossible to pray ; but hope makes our prayers reasonable, passionate, and religious ; for it relies on God's promise. — *Taylor.*

It is good that a man should both hope and quietly wait for the salvation of the Lord.

Hope strengthens, nourishes, and fortifies all the virtues, it softens all afflictions, it weakens all temptations, and is the fruitful source of all good works. — *St. Chrysostom.*

Faith is the substance of things hoped for ; the evidence of things not seen.

Faith, if it be true, living, and justifying, cannot be separated from a good life ; " it overcomes the world," it " works righteousness," and makes us diligently to do, and cheerfully to suffer, whatsoever God hath placed in our way to heaven. — *Taylor.*

Why art thou cast down, O my soul ? and why art thou disquieted within me ? hope in God.

The fear of the Lord is strong confidence ; and his children shall have a place of refuge.

Be of good courage, and he shall strengthen your heart, all that hope in the Lord.

In thee, O Lord, do I hope.

Which hope we have as an anchor of the soul, both sure and steadfast, and which entereth into that within the vail.

MORNING.

OUR Father who art in heaven, thou who art our Creator and daily Preserver, in the morning will we direct our prayer unto thee, and will look up. We thank thee for the repose of another night and for the light of this day. With bodies refreshed by sleep, and with minds awakened anew to the consciousness of existence, we come to thee who art ever watching over us, that we may be taught by thy wisdom and strengthened by thy grace in the duties and labors before us. Our Heavenly Father, we know not what is before us in this day upon which we have entered; but thou knowest, and we feel that thou hast ordered all things for us in mercy and in wisdom. Deepen our faith, we beseech thee, in thy fatherly care and interest. Enable us to feel that thou art ordering our ways, and that thou wilt cause all things to work together for good to them that love thee. O God, we know not what a day may bring forth, or when our appointed time shall come; but we have hope in thee, and in that hope would we abide evermore. Sustained by it, we would do the work which thou hast given us to do in this world, and labor on unto the end, feeling that what thou hast not given us to know here we shall know hereafter. Thou hast assured us, O God, that if we are the obedient disciples of the Lord Jesus Christ in this world, thou wilt receive us into thy bliss in the world to come, and give unto us crowns of righteousness. Having this hope, we would day by day purify ourselves, even as thou art pure, and with diligence and patience seek to fulfil the great end and aim of our being.

Our Heavenly Father, without help from thee we are nothing and can do nothing. Except the Lord build the house, they labor in vain that build it. We trust in thy word, and we feel assured that thou wilt mercifully regard our weaknesses and infirmities, and wilt graciously do for us what we cannot do for ourselves.

Hear us, we beseech thee, in behalf of all those for whom we should pray when we come before the throne of thy grace. May they be the accepted disciples of the Lord Jesus Christ, and daily do thy will. And unto thee shall be given all the praise evermore. *Amen.*

EVENING.

O THOU Infinite and Almighty God, tremblingly, yet gratefully, we bow before thee in this our united, humble prayer. What are we, that we should thus approach the Supreme and Eternal One? And yet, how real the promise that thou wilt hear and welcome all that come to thee! Not with any thought of our own worthiness or desert, but with lowly trust in thy tender and abounding love, we would offer our praise, while we devoutly rejoice before thee in confidence and hope.

Once more the shades of night have fallen around us, and the solemn uncertainty of all life's blessings is forced upon our thought. The darkness of these coming hours is only the symbol of the impenetrable mystery which ever encompasses our path. We know not what of trial or of blessing may be in store in that vast future which lies before us. But we thank thee that, while we cannot penetrate its great uncertainty, we yet can call it ours through faith and hope, and that, whatever of doubt or trial may surround us, hope gives us bright anticipations of joy and of good. Above all, we bless thee that we can have always the expectation of a time when all earthly trials shall be swallowed up in the glad realities of a heavenly state.

And now, O our Father, as we commend ourselves without distrust to thy keeping during the unconsciousness of sleep, so we would resign all our interests and cares to thee. May our rest be soothed and sweetened by the thought of thy presence and the hopes of thy divine and peculiar care. And unto thee, through Jesus Christ, help us to render, now and evermore, grateful and loving praise. *Amen.*

XXXV.

CHRIST WITHIN US.

In vain for thee hath Christ in Bethlehem been born ;
If he 's not born in thee, thy soul is still forlorn.

ANGELUS SILESIUS.

Jesus said, If a man love me, he will keep my words; and my Father will love him, and we will come unto him, and make our abode with him.

If any man have not the Spirit of Christ, he is none of his.

The fruit of the Spirit is love, joy, peace, long-suffering, gentleness, goodness, faith, meekness, temperance.

Examine yourselves, whether ye be in the faith; prove your own selves. Know ye not your own selves, how that Jesus Christ is in you, except ye be reprobates ?

I bow my knees unto the Father of our Lord Jesus Christ.

That Christ may dwell in your hearts by faith; that ye, being rooted and grounded in love, that ye may know the love of Christ that passeth knowledge, that ye might be filled with all the fulness of God.

Behold, I stand at the door and knock; if any man hear my voice, and open the door, I will come in to him, and sup with him, and he with me.

How shall we escape, if we neglect so great salvation.

As ye have, therefore, received Christ Jesus the Lord, so walk ye in him :

Rooted and built up in him, and stablished in the faith.

Morning.

DEAR Father in heaven, who hast sent to us thy holy child Jesus to be our life, grant that to-day he may be life in our souls. May his faith in thee be in us to-day, so that as he saw thee near evermore, we may see thee near evermore. May his perfect trust in thy providential care be in us to-day, that we may feel that thou hast even numbered every hair of our heads. May his devotion to thy will be in our souls, that we also may say, " Not our will, but thine, be done." May his hope of a perfect triumph of right over wrong, good over evil, love over selfishness, truth over error, be also in our souls to-day ; that we may not fear anything which seems defeat or disaster, confident that all things will work together for final and perfect good. So may his Spirit lead our spirits, his thoughts our thoughts, his love our love, and the life we live in the flesh may we live by faith in him, which we ask in his spirit and name. *Amen.*

Evening.

OUR Heavenly Father, thou knowest better than our own hearts know, whether we have employed the hours of this day to the great end for which thou gavest them, — so as to be drawn nearer to thee, to grow more spiritually-minded, to become more like Christ, the Son of thy dear love. As we resign ourselves once more into the tender protection of thy arms, we implore thy forgiveness for every wasted opportunity, every misused privilege, which, had we been faithful, would have brought us closer to thee, and to Christ our Lord.

We thank thee for every holy thought, every moment of communion with thee, every opportunity of faithful and Christian service which we have used this day. Grant, we implore thee, that we may indeed be true branches in Him the living Vine. May his life enter into our lives, his Spirit be infused into our spirits, and we be hid in thee by the mysterious union of believers with Him, our Teacher, Master, Redeemer. Open our hearts to his instructions; touch us so deeply with a sense of his wonderful love, that we may accept his word as the rule of our lives, and be led by his gracious example to an entire and confiding trust in thee. Thou persuadest us by all the discipline of thy providence, by thy voice within our hearts, by the strong attraction of the life of Christ, to follow him in that path where he has gone before us, which leadeth unto thee. O strengthen us against the doubts and fears, the temptations which we put in our own way, and those which the world of pleasure and absorbing care place all around us, — that hinder us continually from following him, and make us deaf to his call. And may he be so formed within us, that we may have that peace which passeth all understanding, and finally may attain to the rest which remaineth for thy people. We ask it in His name. *Amen.*

XXXVI.

VAIN AND EVIL THOUGHTS.

Be with me, Lord, where'er I go ;
Teach me what thou wouldst have me do ;
Suggest whate'er I think or say ;
Direct me in thy narrow way.

CHRISTIAN PSALMIST.

The thought of foolishness is sin : and the scorner is an abomination to men.

Those things which proceed out of the mouth come forth from the heart ; and they defile a man. For out of the heart proceed evil thoughts.

When a good man is afflicted, tempted, or troubled with evil thoughts ; then he understandeth better the great need he hath of God, without whom he perceiveth he can do nothing that is good. — *À Kempis.*

For the word of God is quick and powerful, and sharper than any two-edged sword, piercing even to the dividing asunder of soul and spirit, and of the joints and marrow, and is a discerner of the thoughts and intents of the heart.

Repent, therefore, of thy wickedness, and pray God, if perhaps the thought of thine heart may be forgiven thee.

The thoughts of the wicked are an abomination to the Lord, but the words of the pure are pleasant words.

Charity suffereth long, and is kind; is not easily provoked, thinketh no evil;

Rejoiceth not in iniquity, but rejoiceth in the truth.

Think of good, that you may avoid thinking of evil. The mind of man cannot for one moment remain in a state of inactivity. — *St. Ephraim.*

If thou hast thought evil, lay thine hand upon thy mouth.

Practise to make God thy last thought at night when thou sleepest; and thy first thought in the morning when thou awakest; so shall thy fancy be sanctified in the night, and thy understanding be rectified in the day, so shall thy rest be peaceful and thy labors prosperous. — *Quarles.*

MORNING.

EVER-LIVING God, whose existence is the perpetual spring of our being, and whose loving-kindness is the inspiration of our daily joys: Wilt thou impress our minds with gratitude while we remember thy mercies, and turn our voices to praise while we call upon thy name? By the tender and wise ordering of thy providence, the night has brought us the delightful refreshment of sleep, amid social security and domestic peace; and the welcome radiance of the morning calls us to new activity, to fresh experiences, to a deeper acquaintance with life, and to ever-augmenting responsibilities.

May our hearts be susceptible to every influence that testifies to thy holy presence in the beauty of the world thy hands have fashioned, — in the genial ministries of domestic love and noble friendships, — in the silent witness of a good conscience to the pure thoughts and good deeds that have blessed mankind, — and in every spiritual emotion and aspiration that may ennoble us, by lifting us into a higher realm of life.

O Lord, our Preserver, in guarding our bodies from danger through the day that lies before us, withdraw our eyes from beholding vanity, and exclude from our minds all gross and presumptuous thoughts. May the words which our tongues may utter, and the meditations which our hearts may entertain, be acceptable in thy sight, and worthy the bodies and spirits which thou hast deigned to call thy temple. Here, O God, enthrone thy Holy Spirit, that all our purposes and desires may be subjected to thee; that all our duties may be elevated into privileges; that our pleasures may be exalted into praises; that our forgiven sins may bear the fruit of humility and grateful love; and that the trials of a mortal day, borne to thee on the wings of prayer, may return to us in everlasting benedictions. We ask it through the grace and truth of Jesus Christ. *Amen.*

EVENING.

A T the close of another day, we meet, O Father, to offer unto thee our evening tribute
of thanksgiving, to ask protection through another
night, and to seek our rest in peaceful communion
with thee. It is from thee that all our gifts and
blessings proceed. Thy loving-kindness hath encompassed all our paths, and thy presence of mercy
hath guarded all our sleeping and our waking hours.
We rest this night in the confidence that thou art
our safeguard and our shield.

We thank thee, Father, for the blessings which
this day and all our days have brought to us. We
thank thee for the power of mind and soul which
thou hast bestowed upon us. We thank thee that
thou hast taught us to think wisely, and to feel in
love and at peace with thee and with one another.
We pray thee that all wrong desires and evil
thoughts may be banished from our souls and
minds by the sweet and purifying influence of thy
presence.

Thou, O Father, knowest all the secrets of our
hearts. Before thee our whole being lies open.
There is not a word in our mouth, there is not a
thought in our mind, but lo! thou knowest it altogether. Thou understandest our thoughts afar
off. Search us, we beseech thee, and know our
hearts; try us, and know our thoughts. See if

there be any wicked way in us, and lead us in the way everlasting. May the words of our lips and the meditations of our hearts be acceptable in thy sight, O Father, our Redeemer and our Strength. May the wisdom which is from above, in its purity and its peace, be our perpetual guide. May we be made wise even unto salvation. May all vanity, all malice, all uncharitableness, all evil-speaking, be put far away from us, and may we dwell with thee and with one another in trust and grace and love. Thus guide us through the whole day of our life, and when the night of death shall close around us, may we lie down to sleep amid its shadows, in the hope of awakening in the light of an eternal day with thee. Bless us, Father, and all who are dear to us ; in thine infinite mercy keep, strengthen, and guard us, now and evermore, through **Jesus Christ** our Lord. *Amen.*

XXXVII.

TRUE WISDOM.

Be it my only wisdom here,
To serve the Lord with filial fear
With loving gratitude ;
Superior sense may I display,
By shunning every evil way,
And walking in the good.

WESLEY'S COL.

If any lack of wisdom, let him ask of God, that giveth to all men liberally, and upbraideth not; and it shall be given him.

But let him ask in faith, nothing wavering.

Happy is the man that findeth wisdom, and the man that getteth understanding.

For the merchandise of it is better than the merchandise of silver, and the gain thereof than fine gold.

Take fast hold of instruction ; let her not go ; keep her ; for she is thy life.

Above all, the knowledge of what is good and what is evil, what ought to be done, and what ought not to be done in the several offices and relations of life, is a thing too large to be compassed, and too hard to be mastered, without study and contemplation. — *Dr. South.*

The fear of the Lord is the beginning of wisdom : and the knowledge of the holy is understanding.

Many get no profit of their labor, because they contend for

knowledge rather than for a holy life; and the time shall come when it shall more avail thee to have subdued one lust than to have known all mysteries. — *Taylor.*

Beware lest any man spoil you through philosophy and vain deceit, after the traditions of men, after the rudiments of the world, and not after Christ.

Who is a wise man and endued with knowledge among you? let him show out of a good conversation his words with meekness of wisdom.

The wisdom that is from above is first pure, then peaceable, gentle, and easy to be entreated, full of mercy and good fruits, without partiality and without hypocrisy.

Discover to me, O thou Searcher of hearts, whatever is amiss in me, whether in life or principle. — *Wilson.*

That which I see not, teach Thou me; if I have done iniquity, I will do so no more.

MORNING.

WE thank thee, O most merciful God, that thou hast watched over us, in our helplessness, during the night, and brought us in safety to the beginning of another day. With our renewed powers we would offer new praises to thee. Let our first thoughts be of thy loving-kindness and tender mercy. Let our first acts be those of homage, thanksgiving, and prayer to Him who gave us being, whose goodness never faileth, and whose glory is above the heavens.

Look down upon us, we beseech thee, O Lord, in

7 *

thy great compassion, as we are entering upon an untried day. Let thy blessing follow us as we go forth to the duties which lie before us, — to the enjoyments or the trials which thy providence may have in store for us. If it be thy will, may we walk unharmed through all the dangers and diseases which beset our path. May we pursue our works with safety and success. May we give and receive happiness in our friendly intercourse, and pass our time in rest and quietness of mind. But, O God, grant us above all, and help us to desire before all things, thy best, even thy spiritual gifts. Give us true and heavenly wisdom, — that wisdom which is "first pure, then peaceable, gentle, easy to be entreated, full of mercy and good fruits." The wisdom which guides the soul in the way of thy commandments; which guards the heart from the allurements of sin; which teaches humility, contentment, and gratitude; which finds the true enjoyment of prosperity and the sweet uses of adversity; which, beginning with reverence for God, ends in love both to God and man.

Be this, O Father of lights, thy precious gift to us. Be this the great object of our desire and pursuit to-day. Keep our too inconstant minds from being drawn aside from following after it. Forgive us that we have been, hitherto, so backward and wavering in our endeavors to acquire it. Upbraid us not because we have so little of it. But, O

Lord, for the sake of our need and of thine own
infinite mercy, vouchsafe, from thy fulness, to bestow it upon us in answer to our prayer; which we
humbly present unto thee, with our thanksgivings
and praises, in the name of thy dear Son, Jesus
Christ our Saviour. *Amen.*

EVENING.

OUR Father in heaven, the day is thine, and
the night also is thine. Around the weary
world again thou hast drawn the curtains of darkness. How gracious and constant, and yet how
still, the mighty working of thy providence! Fed
by thy bounty, borne in thine arms, cherished by
thy spirit, what more do we need, what more could
we ask?

If to-day thou hast seen any virtue in us, any
love of truth and willingness to work or to suffer
for it; any fidelity in duty, any devotedness to
thee; O receive our fervent thanksgiving for the
means and opportunity of doing well. And whatever thou hast seen in us to-day unworthy and sinful, O in thy mercy regard it; and may we awake
to see as thou seest, and judge ourselves as thou
judgest us. We ask not so much to be freed from
remorse as from the sin that produces it; not so
much to be overshadowed with peace, as to be
quickened to righteousness, which, in the end, is

full of peace. That peace of God that passeth all understanding, — that peace of the Saviour, which the world can neither give nor take away, — O Father, lead us unto the way of such peace; quicken us by thy Spirit, and lead us to the feet of Christ, that we may learn of him to *live into* thy peaceful, heavenly kingdom.

Father of boundless goodness, let thy blessing rest upon all who are dear to us. O give them wisdom and strength. We pray for ourselves and for all. Forgive us our trespasses as we forgive those who trespass against us, and lead us not into temptation, but deliver us from evil.

O, ever-watchful Guardian, as the night now invites us to sleep and rest, may we commit ourselves to thee, penitent and grateful; and may to-morrow find us nearer to thee than ever before in faith and duty. O hear us as thy children, and as disciples of thy Son. For thine is the kingdom, and the power, and the glory, for ever and ever. *Amen.*

XXXVIII.

THOU, GOD, SEEST US.

Thine all-surrounding sight surveys
My rising and my rest;
My public walks, my private ways,
And secrets of my breast.

So let thy grace surround me still,
And like a bulwark prove,
To guard my soul from every ill,
Secured by sovereign love.

WATTS.

Woe unto them that seek deep to hide their counsel from the Lord, and their works are in the dark, and they say, Who seeth us? and who knoweth us?

Can any hide himself in secret places, that I shall not see him? saith the Lord. Do I not fill heaven and earth? saith the Lord.

The ways of a man are before the eyes of the Lord, and he pondereth all his goings.

Thou hast set our iniquities before thee; our secret sins in the light of thy countenance.

The eyes of the Lord are in every place, beholding the evil and the good.

O Lord, thou hast searched me and known me.

Thou knowest my down-sitting and mine up-rising, thou understandest my thought afar off.

Thou compassest my path and my lying down, and art acquainted with all my ways.

Whither shall I go from thy Spirit? or whither shall I flee from thy presence?

The eyes of the Lord run to and fro throughout the whole earth, to show himself strong in the behalf of them whose heart is perfect towards him.

There is no darkness nor shadow of death where the workers of iniquity may hide themselves.

Therefore he knoweth their works, and he overturneth them, so that they are destroyed.

MORNING.

O GOD, we are still with thee, and we would be still praising thee. We cannot escape thy presence, and we would not escape it, but rejoice and be glad in it. Purify our hearts of every sinful passion and desire, that we may be joyful in thee, that thy presence may fill us with holy reverence and happy, childlike trust. Help us to live to-day as beneath thine eye, conscious that what we do or what we think is alike known to thee. Thus may our life be mingled of fear and love, making us to walk carefully before thee, yet with confidence and peace.

We pray for all those who are dear to us by ties of kindred and affection. Let thy blessed providence and love pursue and keep them. If they are in any trouble, grant them relief and abundant freedom in thee. Pour out thy Spirit upon all men; pity and convert the sinful and wicked; be merciful and full of compassion to the unfortunate; and lead all men to know thee, the only true God, and Jesus Christ, whom thou hast sent. And may thy will be done on earth as it is in heaven. *Amen.*

EVENING.

O GOD, we come to thee, who encompassest all our ways. As the shadows of evening close around us, thine eye beholds us still. Even the night is light about us. The darkness and the light are both alike to thee. With reverence and awe we remember that thou lookest through every veil which conceals the secrets of our hearts from the world or from ourselves, and knowest every thought of passion or of sin. Thou seest the hidden stains which have not been revealed to us. O Thou, in whose sight the heavens are not clean, how unutterably impure must our weak, straying, selfish hearts appear to thee! Look upon us in thy infinite pity, as well as in thy infinite purity. We rejoice to know that thou not only seest every thought of sin, but also every thought of purity. Every secret struggle against temptation is open to thine eye; every silent prayer is heard before thy throne; and thou wilt hasten to send thy assisting angels to strengthen these faint aspirations for light and life, and to kindle every spark of holier feeling into a constant flame of love.

All-merciful Father, amidst our confessions of weakness, we give thanks that we are beneath thine all-seeing eye. Thou canst discern our spirits' inmost need. Thou wilt rebuke every frailty, and humble every thought of pride, and break down every impenitent desire, and never leave nor forsake thy often-straying child. Make these thoughts our hope and trust. Give us the lowly confidence which desires to lay open every secret weakness to thee. Grant the love which casts out fear. Help us, in the spirit of our Master and Lord, always to realize thy immediate and guardian presence, as our perpetual inspiration and sure defence. Then shall we begin to see thee as thou seest us, and find the light of thy countenance cheering every path of life, and illuminating the valley of the shadow of death. Help us thus to see thee in that infinite mercy revealed through Jesus Christ our Lord. *Amen.*

XXXIX.

AGAINST PRIDE.

Wherefore should man, frail child of clay,
Who, from his cradle to the shroud,
Lives but the insect of a day, —
O why should mortal man be proud?

By doubt perplexed, in error lost,
With trembling step he seeks his way:
How vain of wisdom's gift the boast!
Of reason's lamp, how faint the ray!
ENFIELD.

Pride goeth before destruction, and an haughty spirit before a fall.

The fear of the Lord is the instruction of wisdom; and before honor is humility.

Thus saith the high and lofty One that inhabiteth eternity, whose name is Holy: I dwell in the high and holy place, with him also that is of a contrite and humble spirit.

Humility is truth, and Pride a lie: the one glorifies God, the other dishonors him. Humility makes men to be like angels, Pride makes angels to become devils. — *Taylor.*

Pride is folly, Humility is the temper of a holy spirit and excellent wisdom. Humility is the way to glory, Pride to ruin and confusion. — *Taylor.*

God resisteth the proud, but giveth grace to the humble.

If a man thinketh himself to be something, when he is nothing, he deceiveth himself.

But let every man prove his own work, and then shall he have rejoicing in himself alone, and not in another.

Whosoever shall exalt himself shall be abased; and he that shall humble himself, shall be exalted.

A man's pride shall bring him low; but honor shall uphold the humble in spirit.

Let us never forget that the day will come when all our virtues will be tried as by fire, and that this fire humility alone will be able to withstand. — *St. Ephraim.*

Morning.

ALMIGHTY God, who art exalted above all height, look down, we beseech thee, in tender compassion, upon us, thy weak and erring and sinning children, while in prostration of spirit we bow down before thee, and offer unto thee our morning sacrifice. We acknowledge our dependence; we confess our sins; we ask thy forgiveness and thy succor. Help us, O God, to feel our weakness and our unworthiness. Help us to know ourselves, how ignorant and frail and sinful we are; how oft we have offended, how far short we have come of our duty and of thy just requirements. O help us to suppress all presumptuous thoughts, all vanity and pride, all self-seeking and all undue self-reliance; and let us learn the hard lesson of self-renunciation, so that, whatever good thing we may do, whatever attainments we make, we may be ever ready to say,

" Not unto us, O Lord, not unto us, but unto thy name, be all the glory and all the praise.

Great and manifold have been thy acts of loving-kindness towards us. O, how poor and imperfect have been the returns we have made! Help us, our Heavenly Father, to renounce all spiritual pride, and may we be clothed with humility. Create within us a new heart, — a heart that aspires to thee, and that finds its peace in thee. Renew within us a right spirit, — that spirit of filial love which shall draw us to thee, and make obedience a willing service.

Help us to cultivate that lowliness of mind that shall exclude all arrogance and boasting, and shall lead us to render to every man his due. Let us not look with envy upon those above, nor with contempt upon those below us, but honor all men as thy children and our brothers; and, forgetting the things that are behind, and reaching forth to those things that are before, may we press toward the mark, and reach the prize of our high calling in Christ Jesus our Lord. *Amen.*

EVENING.

ALMIGHTY God, who hast given the day for labor, the evening for meditation, and the night for repose, we would glorify thee for all thy gifts, and remember in praise the divine care that always remembers us in mercy. For all the opportunities of the past day, we desire to thank thee. If we have improved them by honesty and diligence, we seek our highest reward in thy approbation, confirmed by a quiet conscience. If we have been negligent or unfaithful, we would not avert the condemnation of thy just law; but would see in the cloud of thy judgment the admonition of a righteous wisdom, and strive again, with returning day, for the prize of our high calling in Jesus Christ.

For all the advantages we possess, and for all the pure pleasures we enjoy, as individuals and as a Christian household, may we remember the Perfect and Liberal Giver. Yet forbid, O God, that we should esteem ourselves more highly than we ought, or foster a presumptuous and arrogant spirit. We have nothing but what thy favor and love have bestowed, — no grace or charm of person, no power of mind or eminence of station, but what thou hast lent us, to subserve thy holy purpose. Nor have we anything of which thy just judgments may not deprive us, if our spiritual good require that our hearts be humbled and our fortune abased. Temper us, then, with a becoming humility of spirit, and may we never abuse the favors with which thy lavish kindness crowns our days.

And now, O Father, through the solemnity of

this night, let thy good providence guard cur repose, and thy Holy Spirit distil into our weary minds the balm of heavenly peace. And, while the heavens that bend over us reveal thy glory, may we close our eyes in conscious security, feeling that we are always with thee, — the greatest and best of Beings, — and that all the families of the earth may put their trust under the shelter of thy love. *Amen.*

XL.

DILIGENT IN BUSINESS.

The works my calling doth propose,
Let me not idly shun ;
For he whom idleness undoes,
Is more than twice undone !
If my estate enlarge, I may
Enlarge my love to thee ;
And though I more and more decay,
Yet let me thankful be.
                              WITHER.

Walk worthy of the vocation wherewith ye are called.

Seest thou a man diligent in his business? he shall stand before kings.

Study to be quiet, and to do your own business, and to work with your own hands,

That ye may walk honestly toward them that are without, and that ye may have lack of nothing.

It is good and comely for one to eat and to drink, and to enjoy the good of all his labor that he taketh under the sun all the days of his life, which God giveth him; for it is his portion.

When we were with you, this we commanded you, that if any would not work, neither should he eat.

He becometh poor that dealeth with a slack hand; but the hand of the diligent maketh rich.

He that gathereth in summer is a wise son; but he that sleepeth in harvest is a son that causeth shame.

He that is slothful in his work is brother to him that is a great waster.

Slothfulness casteth into a deep sleep; and an idle soul shall suffer hunger.

From the beginning God has made it a law to man to labor; not as a punishment and trouble, but as an exercise and instruction. — *St. Chrysostom.*

Poverty and labor make more saints than wealth and idleness. — *St. Chrysostom.*

Go to the ant, consider her ways and be wise:

Which, having no guide, overseer, or ruler, provideth her meat in the summer and gathereth her food in the harvest.

MORNING.

WE thank thee, O God, for the return of light. Renewed by sleep and rest, we find

ourselves surrounded by thy care and love. With
uplifted hearts would we accept the great gifts
which come to us in a day of life, — gifts of
bounty, and thought, and love, and home, — gifts
of faith and hope.

Give us wisdom, we beseech thee, for the work
before us to-day. May we give it dignity and
sacredness by the spirit in which we do it. Now is
the accepted time, now the day of our salvation.
To-day it is given us to come nearer to thee and
the blessed immortality, and the business that waits
for us should be our preparation and discipline. O
keep us from wrong-doing; may we engage in no
enterprise upon which thy blessing may not rest.
Aid us to deal justly, to love mercy, and to walk
humbly before thee. May the words of thy Son be
our rule, — to do to others as we would have them
do to us. O may the Spirit of Christ be in us,
that like him we may be meek if injured, patient
if tried, courageous if in the face of dangers, and
waiting upon thy will at all times.

May thy blessing rest on all those who go forth,
in these morning hours, into the various paths of
business. May they carry religion into all their
work, — fellow-laborers with thee, may they recognize thy mighty agencies in earth, and air, and
water, as helpers in their work. May we all consider that our strength, thought, ingenuity, are thy
gifts, and whatever we do, may it be done for the

welfare of humanity, and for thy glory. May thy kingdom come, and thy will be done on earth as it is in heaven.

Hear us, O Heavenly Father, in our morning prayer, hear us as disciples of thy Son, and thine be the praise, world without end. *Amen.*

EVENING.

O THOU infinite and holy God, we devoutly thank thee for that providence which has guided and kept us through another day. May we remember thy mercies with gratitude, and strive to keep thy most holy law. As darkness falls on the earth, and we lay ourselves down to sleep, wilt thou keep us in safety. What we have done this day which meets with thine approval, wilt thou bless. Forgive us wherein we have done wrong, or have omitted to do that which we ought to have done. We would now examine our hearts. If we have toiled with cheerfulness and fidelity, if we have carried a devout frame of mind into our calling, if we have been truthful to our fellow-men, kind and unselfish in the family, may we have the smile of thine approval. Grant that we may know our thoughts, and see if there be any wicked feeling within us, or any wrong habit in our lives, and may we be led through penitence and faith into the way everlasting. We thank thee that thou art leading us to a fuller knowledge of thy most perfect will. Thou hast appointed that man should go forth to labor; if, in thy providence, this labor has been rewarded with an increase of worldly goods, may this enlarge our hearts, and prompt us to make a wise and faithful use of thy gracious gifts. In our abundance may we remember the poor and needy, and manifest our gratitude to thee by acts of kindly charity and beneficence. Even if misfortune has overtaken us, may we learn obedience to thy dispensations, and through the experience of adversity gain imperishable riches. Thou, O Lord, givest, and thou takest away. May we accept the condition of our lives with uncomplaining thankfulness, and perform all our duties with diligence and fidelity, so that when life shall end, and we pass through the valley of the shadow of death, we may hear the Saviour's welcome, " Well done, good and faithful servant, enter thou into the joy of the Lord." All for which we pray as disciples of thy Son, our Lord and Saviour Jesus Christ. *Amen.*

XLI.

GOOD EXAMPLE.

No act falls fruitless; none can tell
How vast its power may be;
Nor what results enfolded dwell
Within it, silently.
LONDON INQUIRER.

So live with men as considering always that God sees thee. — *Anon.*

Let your light so shine before men, that they may see your good works, and glorify your Father which is in heaven.

Be thou an example of the believers, in word, in conversation, in charity, in spirit, in faith, in purity.

Take heed lest by any means ye become a stumbling-block to them that are weak.

If meat make my brother to offend, I will eat no flesh while the world standeth, lest I make my brother to offend.

Let us consider one another, to provoke unto love and to good works.

In all things showing thyself a pattern of good works; in doctrine showing uncorruptness, gravity, sincerity, sound speech that cannot be denied:

That he that is of the contrary part may be ashamed, having no evil thing to say of you.

Know, that he which converteth the sinner from the error of his way shall save a soul from death, and shall hide a multitude of sins.

Be instant in season and out of season; reprove, rebuke, exhort, with all long-suffering and doctrine.

When a man's ways please the Lord, he maketh even his enemies to be at peace with him.

The path of the just is as the shining light, which shineth more and more unto the perfect day.

MORNING.

BEFORE thee, the ever-merciful Father, ever mindful of our wants, we come to renew our worship this morning. By thy power is the blessed light of the day again brought to our eyes; by thy goodness is our strength renewed; by thy mercy are many blessings preserved to us; and by thy kind providence are the duties which now lie before us appointed.

And we thank thee, our Heavenly Father, not only for the gifts of thy bounty, by which comfort is multiplied in our home, but also for the duties which each day brings to us. We know that thou hast ordained these duties that we might be blessed in the fulfilment of them; and that thou hast given us no commandments which are grievous.

May we, then, be grateful for our opportunities for bearing witness to what we believe to be true and right, and for our opportunities of doing good, in all ways, to our fellow-beings. May we strengthen each others' minds and hearts in every good word and work. May no reproach be brought, by our lips or lives, upon our Saviour's cause. Make us faithful to our privileges of sympathy and fellowship with all who call upon thy name through Jesus Christ. Assist us always to receive from them, and to impart to them, some quickening of Christian faith, some renewing of patience, courage, and hope. Suffer not thy children's sincere and humble strivings to know and do thy will to be in vain; but, through thy Spirit helping our infirmities, may we ever promote thy kingdom of righteousness, truth, and peace. *Amen.*

.

EVENING.

FATHER of mercies, it is in thy mercy that we come to the close of this day, and look back upon a day which thou hast blessed. We thank thee for the life which thou hast given us, for thy constant presence and direction, for thy love, binding us to each other and to thee. We trust it has brought us nearer thee, nearer to the heavenly life, as it has brought us nearer to the end of our lives upon the earth. We trust that we have by no act led any fellow-being astray; that our example has been good, and not evil. For what we have left undone forgive us, and show us our shortcomings, that in the days to come we may repair them. For what the day has brought us, receive our repeated thanks, and help us use those gifts in thy service by devoting them to our brothers and sisters in the world. And now bless us and keep us, as we close our eyes in slumber, and mercifully protect us through the darkness of the night. We ask it in the name of our Lord and Saviour. *Amen.*

XLII.

THE WORD OF GOD.

Word of the ever-living God;
Will of his glorious Son!
Without thee how could earth be trod,
Or heaven itself be won?

BARTON.

The word of God is quick and powerful, and sharper than any two-edged sword, piercing even to the dividing asunder of soul and spirit, and of the joints and marrow, and is a discerner of the thoughts and intents of the heart.

There is but one book in the world that makes religion consist in loving God more than ourselves, and renouncing self for him; all others that repeat this great truth are borrowed from this, all truth is taught in this fundamental truth. — *Fénelon.*

Jesus said, My mother and my brethren are these which hear the word of God and do it.

But be ye doers of the word, and not hearers only, deceiving your own selves.

I will meditate in thy precepts, and have respects unto thy ways.

I will delight myself in thy statutes; I will not forget thy word.

Thy word is a lamp unto my feet, and a light unto my path.

The Gospel will not be a means of salvation to him who reads and hears it only, but to him who reads, loves, remembers, and practises it by a lively faith. — *Wilson.*

Blessed are the undefiled in the way, who walk in the law of the Lord.

Blessed are they who keep his testimonies, and that seek him with the whole heart.

Grant me, O God, rightly to understand, and constantly to walk in the way of thy commandments. — *Wilson.*

Teach me thy statutes. Incline my heart unto thy testimonies.

Then shall I not be ashamed when I have respect unto all thy commandments.

MORNING.

WE thank thee, O Lord, our Heavenly Father, for thy watchful care over us through another night. Thine eye, which never slumbers, hath guarded our unconscious hours, and we begin our life anew, because of the freshness of thy reviving influence. Breathe upon us and through us, in these morning hours, and guide us through the day. Give unto us all things which may be needful for our good. Keep away from us all things evil. Be our help in every temptation, our strength in every duty, and our consolation in every grief.

We thank thee that thou hast taught us of thyself, and thy wonderful providence, by thy works and by thy word. We call thee Father. We would be as thy children before thee. We thank thee for the life and teachings of Him who hath shown us the Father. We desire to feel his love upon and in our hearts, and we desire to feel our hearts going out to him in love. We recognize in his person our Master, Lord, and Saviour. We hear the words of heavenly wisdom that drop from his lips. We witness the beauty, the excellence, the divineness, of his life. We feel the inflowings of his Spirit in our souls.

Jesus Christ hath taught us that we are to love thee with all our hearts, and all our minds, and all our souls, and all our strength. Second only to thyself within us, would we cherish the love of our Redeemer. We would call to mind the struggles and conflicts through which he passed, the toils which he bore, the pains which he endured, and the sacrifices which he made for us. We are healed by his stripes, and in his death we live. Help us, then, O Father, to become his true disciples and his faithful followers. We would sit at his feet, and learn of him the wisdom which is for our salvation. We would endure all grief and pain with the trust which was his source of strength. We would meet all difficulty and danger with the courage by which he was upborne. We would lie down to death with the willing and submissive faith in thee which glorified his cross. May we thus live and die through him, and through him enter upon that holier life, and dwell in that eternal house, whose mansions he hath prepared for us. And unto thee, his Father and our Father, be praise and thanksgiving forevermore. *Amen.*

Evening.

O THOU infinite, ever-present Spirit, Source of all wisdom and intelligence, whose inspiration giveth understanding, who enlightenest every man that cometh into the world! we thank thee for all our powers and capacities, and for all the gifts thou hast bestowed upon thy rational offspring. We thank thee for all the revelations thou hast made of thyself in the past ages, and for such as thou art making to us continually. The heavens declare thy glory. Day unto day and night unto night bear witness to thy eternal power and godhead. In the light of reason and in the power of conscience, we would gratefully recognize thy Spirit, teaching, warning, and guiding us, and leading us to thee.

But above all do we thank thee for the written

Word, — the word spoken by prophets, and seers, and holy men of old, that has come down to us through the ages, speaking to us as it spake to the fathers, shedding light upon the nations. Especially do we thank thee for the Word manifest in the flesh, — for the gift of thy dear Son, and the redemption of the world, purchased by his blood. At his feet we would reverently sit and learn of him. As he spake with a divine authority, may we receive with humble and teachable minds the truth to which he bore witness, and may the truth make us free indeed. Let it not be our condemnation, that we have slighted his message, or withheld from him the honor due to his name. And following him, who is the Way, and the Truth, and the Life, may we find a true peace, and finally enter into that rest that remaineth for the people of God. *Amen.*

XLIII.

THE END OF LIFE.

Lord, what is life? — if spent with thee,
In humble praise and prayer,
How long or short its date may be,
We feel no anxious care;
Though life depart, our joys shall last
When time and all its joys are past.

J. Taylor.

The more we sink into the infirmities of age, the nearer we are to immortal youth. — *Collier.*

The present time is but the infancy of life; its maturity, its perfection, is not in this world. — *St. Gregory.*

Lord make me to know mine end, and the measure of my days, what it is; that I may know how frail I am.

The wages of sin is death; but the gift of God is eternal life, through Jesus Christ our Lord.

There is no death for those who die in Christ, there is only sleep. Can they dread the arrival of that which forever sets them free from sin, and all its cruel snares? — *St. Ephraim.*

For we krow that if our earthly house of this tabernacle were dissolved, we have a building of God, an house not made with hands, eternal in the heavens.

Only let your conversation be as becometh the gospel of Christ; that ye stand fast in one spirit, with one mind striving together for the faith of the gospel.

When the fruit is ripe, it falls off the tree easily. So when a Christian's heart is truly weaned from the world, h.s is prepared for death. — *Anon.*

They that spend their days in faith and prayer, shall end their days in peace and comfort. — *J. Mason.*

For godliness is profitable unto. all things, having promise of the life that now is, and of that which is to come.

MORNING.

EVER–LIVING and ever-present God, our Heavenly Father, we thank thee for the life and immortality brought to light by Jesus Christ our Lord. We thank thee that, though he was made subject unto death, as we are, it was witnessed, by his resurrection, that over him death had no power. And since, in thine all-wise providence, it was ordained that our human life should be always subject to uncertainty, and that to none shall this world be a final home, may we ever look at the things which are unseen and eternal in the heavens. We would not judge for ourselves, or for those dearest to us, concerning the time of continuance here. In thy hand are all souls. Whenever, to us or to our friends, the last of earth shall come, may we be found doing thy work and obedient to thy will. Take away from our hearts, O Father, everything that doth separate us from thee. May we be thine wholly. May our earthly affections and friendships be so sanctified by Christian faith, that they may

continue, uninterrupted by death, abiding forevermore in heaven. May the things of the unseen
future always be to us as present realities. While
we remain on earth, may we grow in the love of
thyself, and of all the holy things which we hope to
love forever. And finally, of thy great mercy, wilt
thou, in thine own time, call us to thyself; which
we ask in the name of Christ, our Lord. *Amen.*

Evening.

GRANT, most merciful Father, that thy gracious benediction may rest upon us now at the
close of this day. We thank thee for the comforts,
the privileges, and the duties which it has offered to
us. Forgive us, if we have failed to use them as
we ought. And help us to be more diligent in all
time to come, that every setting sun may awaken in
us a new sense of thy favor, and bear witness to
our growth in grace, and in the knowledge of our
Lord Jesus Christ, and that every day, in its finished labors, may prepare us for the night in which
no man can work. Open to us wider and truer
views of thyself. May we attain to a more satis-
fying and heavenly wisdom. May we live in closer
and more endearing intimacy with thee. May our
affections be refined and ripened, day by day, for
the kingdom of heaven. May every new joy or
sorrow, every new event or experience, so draw us

to thee, and so fulfil for us the great and holy ends of life, that, day by day, we may be lifted up into higher realms of thought, that we may love thee with a more perfect love, that we may be transformed more and more into the image of our Lord, and that when earthly interests and friends pass from us, heavenly hopes, affections, and companionships may gain new power over us, and make it easy for us to leave all that we possess here, and pass on, with thy peace in our hearts, from the things which are seen and temporal to the things which are unseen and eternal. So may the closing days of life, enriched by gracious memories and immortal hopes, be serene and holy. And at last, through thine infinite mercy, may we be numbered with those of whom thou hast said, " Blessed are the dead which die in the Lord ; for they rest from their labors and their works do follow them." Even so, most holy and merciful Father, through thy great mercy in Him who gave himself for us, and died that we might live. *Amen.*

XLIV.

DAILY FAULTS.

The cheapest sins most dearly punished are,
Because to shun them also is so cheap;
For we have wit to mark them, and to spare.
O crumble not away thy soul's fair heap!

HERBERT.

Small offences become great in our eyes, as the light of God increases within us. — *Fénelon.*

We must condemn our faults, lament them, repent of them, without seeking any palliation or excuse, viewing ourselves as in the presence of God. — *Fénelon.*

Cleanse thou me from secret faults. Keep back thy servant also from presumptuous sins.

Confess your faults one to another, and pray one for another, that ye may be healed.

Now, therefore, thus saith the Lord of hosts, Consider your ways.

For I know your manifold transgressions and your sins. Seek good, and not evil, that ye may live.

Have mercy upon me, O Lord; for I am weak: O Lord, heal me.

It is at its source that evil must be stopped; even though it may not arrive immediately at its height, it must not on that account be neglected. It will grow during your sleep; it is only a germ, but if you do not extirpate it, it will bring forth the fruits of death. — *St. John Chrysostom.*

Beware how you regard as trifling, faults which appear of but little consequence. An accumulation of small faults makes a very large one; grains of sand, gathered together one upon another, form the banks on which the vessel strikes. — *St. Augustine.*

Little sins do greatly deface the image of God in the soul. — *Hopkins.*

MORNING.

WE would acknowledge, O God, with gratitude, thine unmeasured and immeasurable love, which daily renews our life, and daily gives us the means to gain wisdom and virtue. Help us to show our gratitude by consecrating ourselves to thy service, — to thy service, which alone is perfect freedom, in which alone is real life. Help us, O Father, this day, to make the word of Jesus our guide and standard; help us so to live that his word may not condemn us in the hour of judgment. We confess that his yoke is easy and his burden light; and that we are most unreasonable in our disobedience, doing wrong on slight temptation; whilst thou hast given us, in his precious promises, and equally precious warnings, the strongest motives to resist the tempter. But he bade us ask for the gifts of the Holy Spirit, and we therefore pray thee for its gracious influences. We know that it will add to our guilt if we sin against thy good Spirit. But may the very thought that thou art with us and helping us be our strength in duty and our defence against temptation. Let us not deceive ourselves with the vain hope that our sins can be deemed small because done upon small temptation, or pardonable because we constantly repeat them. Bring to our remembrance, according to our Lord's promise, his words in all their awful strictness, binding us to govern every word and every thought; and also in all their glorious riches of mercy, promising forgiveness always to the penitent and obedient spirit; and may his word become in us the fountain of everlasting life. We thank thee that thou hast through him offered us eternal life and blessedness; suffer us not, O gracious God, to waste our daily opportunities for gaining the crown of life; suffer us not, by what we may deem little sins, to exchange our heavenly inheritance for a heritage of everlasting shame.

And these blessings of thy grace we would ask not only for ourselves, but for all who are dear to us; for our neighbors also, and for all mankind. Give thy word, O God, this day success in every land. Establish righteousness upon the earth, and cast wickedness out of her high places. Confound the counsels of the ungodly, and bring them to naught, but let thy church be sanctified, and be extended until the world is filled with thy glory. *Amen.*

EVENING.

O GOD, thou Searcher of hearts, we mourn that our faults are so stubborn and abiding, and that, often as we discover and lament them and strive against them, they do still so mightily return upon us. Let us make honest confession of this our frailty, and be willing to appear at thy mercy-seat just as we are, without pretence or reserve. Thou canst know us, and yet pity, forgive, and save.

Help us, O Father, to study more deeply and humbly the springs of our perversity, that we may know our own frailties so wisely as to trace them to their source, and find their cure. Save us, All-Merciful, from despairing over our own sins, and graciously give us comforting views of our own gifts and thy graces, that we may be encouraged to overcome the evil that is within us with thine abounding good. Save us from all such desponding views of ourselves as tend to quench the spirit of hope, and enable us in the hour of darkness and temptation to cling to thy mercy-seat, and to claim the comforts of thy love.

Help us, O God, to watch and pray that we may not enter into temptation. Help us to resist the least beginning of evil, and so to set a guard upon our eyes and lips and walk, as to keep us from every occasion of sin and open every pathway of rectitude.

And O, blessed God, Giver of all good, Com forter in all trouble, Renewer of souls, in thy loving-kindness open unto us the fountains of heavenly wisdom and power, that we may repel all evil spirits and tempers by the angels of grace, and the life that is born of thy Holy Spirit may overcome the life of sin and death.

All glory be to thee for thy long-suffering mercy, thy forbearance with our miserable frailties, and make us strong and holy by a righteousness better than our own, even through thy beloved Son, Jesus Christ. *Amen.*

XLV.

PURE RELIGION AND UNDEFILED.

> *The uplifted eye and bended knee*
> *Are but vain homage, Lord, to thee;*
> *In vain our lips thy praise prolong,*
> *The heart a stranger to the song.*
> SCOTT.

If any man seem to be religious, and bridleth not his tongue, but deceiveth his own heart, this man's religion is vain.

Pure religion and undefiled before God and the Father is this, To visit the fatherless and widows in their affliction, and to keep himself unspotted from the world.

Religion was not intended to minister to fame and reputation, but to pardon of sins, to the pleasure of God, and the salvation of souls. — *Taylor.*

The Lord knoweth them that are his. Let every one that nameth the name of Christ depart from iniquity.

Virtue does not consist in avoiding evil, through fear of chastisement, like a slave;

Nor in doing good solely with a view to recompense, like a merchant carrying on his traffic;

But to do it without even thinking of the rewards promised to us for it in another life; without fearing anything but estrangement from God; without desiring anything but the sole good of knowing Him, and being united to Him, in his love. — *St. Gregory of Nyssa.*

Vice stings us even in our pleasures, but virtue consoles us even in our pains. — *Colton.*

Blessed are they which do hunger and thirst after righteousness; for they shall be filled.

For I say unto you, that except your righteousness shall exceed the righteousness of the scribes and Pharisees, ye shall in no case enter into the kingdom of heaven.

Be ye therefore perfect, even as your Father which is in heaven is perfect.

MORNING.

O THOU who art the Giver of life, and of everything which makes life a blessing! before entering on our daily cares and duties, we would again look up for that light and help from above which we so much need.

Confirm and strengthen every good purpose of our souls. May we remember that to obey the gospel is the best way to possess it; that it is not the bended knee, but the pure thought, the upright intention, the large and generous heart, the unspotted life, which finds favor with thee. To be followers of Him who is set forth as our Example and Lord, we must walk reverently and patiently in his steps, making it our meat to do the will of our Heavenly Father, and to finish his work.

O God, if amidst our domestic anxieties, or in the excitements and perplexities of business, we should at any time this day forget thee, we beseech thee to have pity on us, to reclaim us to a sense of thy presence, and lead us in the way of eternal life: for thine is the kingdom, and the power, and the glory, forever. *Amen.*

EVENING.

O GOD, thy goodness is new every morning, and fresh every evening. All creatures wait on thee, and thou givest them their meat in due season. We have gone forth to-day under thy care and providence, and now we look to thee for that rest which our bodies need, and for thy gracious benediction upon our hearts. We thank thee for thy care through the day; that we have been permitted to engage in our accustomed duties; that we have found activity, satisfaction, and happiness in them. Teach us, O God, how our daily labors may be made the school of our souls, — a discipline of patience, truth, and purity. May we remember that the temptations of life are in our own hearts, and not in any of the things of this world that God hath made. Thou canst not be tempted, neither temptest thou any man. Purify our hearts by thy blessed Spirit, that we may serve thee truly in making all our duties a spiritual service unto thee. Save us from the mistake of setting a part of our duty for the whole of it. Thou requirest of us, not only to do good, but to walk reverently before God. Help us to keep this holy equity of soul, that our earthly life may be so blended with heavenly temper, that all things may have a moral and spiritual intent to our patient, believing hearts. May we write thy whole law upon our hearts, and may it have its blessed success in our daily living. Help us to be just, merciful, and pure. May we not incline to one of these, and omit the others, but may we remember that pure and undefiled religion before God is to keep them all. May these reverent and humble thoughts sink deep into our hearts, and when the morning light shall come, may they appear in courageous, devout, and godly living. *Amen.*

XLVI.

AGAINST WORLDLY-MINDEDNESS.

Instruct thou me, O God!
And give me grace to heed
With what vain things ourselves we load,
And what we rather need.
                                        WITHER.

Love not the world, nor the things that are in the world; if any man love the world, the love of the Father is not in him.

Give me, O God, the eyes of faith, that I may see the world just as it is; — the vanity of its promises, the folly of its pleasures, the unprofitableness of its rewards, the multitude of its snares, and the dangers of its temptations. — *Wilson.*

Set your affections on things above, not on things on the earth.

What terror, what affliction, can equal that of a Christian, who has never thought of weaning his heart from the world till he comes to die. — *Wilson.*

Although thou shouldest possess all created good, yet couldest thou not be happy thereby nor blessed; but in God, who created all things, consisteth thy whole blessedness and felicity. — *À Kempis.*

Learn so to look upon the honors, the pomp, and greatness of the world, as to look through them. — *South.*

For the wisdom of this world is foolishness with God.

Surely every man walketh in a vain show; surely they are disquieted in vain; he heapeth up riches, and knoweth not who shall gather them.

He that loveth silver shall not be satisfied with silver; nor he that loveth abundance with increase.

Lay up for yourselves treasures in heaven, where neither moth nor rust doth corrupt, and where thieves do not break through nor steal.

For where your treasure is there will your heart be also.

MORNING.

OUR Father in Heaven, we thank thee for the return of this morning, and for the renewal of our daily blessings. We love to feel that we are always surrounded by thee, and that the blessings of each day are the gifts of thy providence. We love to feel that thou art coming to us in the joy and freshness of the morning, in the serenity and peace of the evening, in the love of our loved ones, in the happiness of our home, in the discipline of daily experience, and in all things which make us glad, and strong, and heavenly-minded. And now, before entering upon the labors and trials of this day, we meet together that we may think how real and earnest life should be; how innocently and actively we should enter into it, and how much we need thy guidance, even when we cannot think of thee. O Lord, how often have we felt that we

would be more obedient to all thy commands!
How often have we said within ourselves, "This
day we will not sin ; we will be kind, and just, and
patient, and affectionate all day, and lie down at
night without a regretful memory!" But alas! as
the excitements of duty or pleasure come upon us,
we grow anxious and restless, or forgetful and friv-
olous, and find at the close of the day that we are
careful and troubled about many things, and that
we have not yet found that "good part" which cannot thus be taken away from us. Our Heavenly
Father, we now come to thee with no confidence in
our own strength, and pray that thou wilt help us.
Let thy grace be sufficient for us. Come to us
many times this day, in holy thought and reverent
feeling, and thus keep us near thee, even in our
forgetfulness. May all that is beautiful remind us
of thee, the infinite Beauty. May all that is lovely
remind us of thee, the One altogether lovely.
May all that is true lead us to thee, the Source of
all truth. O, send us not from thy presence un-
blessed ; but breathe thy loving Spirit upon us all
before we take up the burden of our daily duty,
that we may go on our way rejoicing, and the
words of our mouths and the meditations of our
hearts may be acceptable in thy sight, O Lord,
our Strength and our Redeemer. *Amen.*

EVENING.

FATHER, our minds are unquiet because they are full of worldly thoughts and fears. Our worldly thoughts drive out the thought of thee and of thy Son, — drive out peace and contentment, — and we cannot be at rest with thee or in ourselves till these are gone.

Therefore, O Father, we pray thee to take away these thoughts out of our hearts, — these desolate thoughts, which refuse consolation, which seek death instead of life, sin instead of goodness, and lies instead of truth.

O most pitiful One, destroy in us the insatiable desire for pleasure, the burning love of wealth, — destroy this thirst, never satisfied, which brings affliction in the day and fear in the night; which makes us poorer, the richer we become; which rises in the morning for gain, and dreams at night of gold.

Destroy, O God, this love of outward things for themselves; let us love them only as coming from thee, and as giving us the means of helping others. May thy gifts be for others' good, and all as trusts for which we are to account. May we not trust in them, but in thee, and use them as not abusing them always. *Amen.*

XLVII.

LOVE TOWARDS GOD.

My soul, inspired with sacred love,
God's holy name forever bless;
Of all his favors mindful prove,
And still thy grateful thanks express.

TATE AND BRADY.

Thou shalt love the Lord thy God with all thine heart, and with all thy soul, and with all thy might.

And this is love, that we walk after his commandments.

To love God is to make his will ours; it is to obey faithfully his laws; it is to abhor sin. — *Fénelon.*

The true love of God regulates and inspires all our attachments. We never love our neighbor so truly as when our love for him is prompted by the love of God. — *Fénelon.*

O God, reign in our hearts; let the flame of thy holy love extinguish all other. — *Fénelon.*

I will love thee, O Lord, my strength.

Great peace have they that love thy law, and nothing shall offend them.

The Lord preserveth all them that love him.

Acquaint now thyself with him, and be at peace: thereby good shall come unto thee.

God keepeth covenant and mercy for them that love him and observe his commandments.

There is no fear in love; but perfect love casteth out all fear.

See, I have set before thee this day life and good, and death and evil;

In that I have commanded thee this day to love the Lord your God, to walk in his ways, and to keep his commandments and his statutes and his judgments.

MORNING.

OUR Father, who art in heaven, thy children praise thee for the sleep of the night, and its rest and blessing, and for the light and beauty of the morning. Be pleased to come home to us through this day, that we may spend it as those should who live and move and have their being in their God. Renew within us our love and reverence for thee. Remind us often of thy presence, that we may often be grateful for thy love. Whenever we are afraid, give us courage; whenever we are weary, give us strength; whenever we are cast down, give us hope; and show us in all things how to do the work that thou shalt give into our hands. And so when we are glad this day, make us more glad because thou art with us, and in all our pleasures let us thank thee, the Giver. We offer all our prayers in our dear Master's name. *Amen.*

EVENING.

EVER-PRESENT Friend, we bow before thee in lowly thanksgiving and grateful thought this evening, remembering and feeling all thy love. For all thy gifts this day we thank thee; for the life of our bodies, and the undying life of our souls, which thou art renewing; for bodily health and strength, and for mental and spiritual strength; for all our powers of feeling, thought, and action. Again we thank thee for the surroundings of home, neighborhood, citizenship; for the relations of affection, of labor, or friendship. Each day, as it comes to us, is a rich gift, full of precious presents, — full of opportunities by which we can learn more, do more, and love more. May all lead us to love thee, — the Fountain of every good and every precious and perfect gift. Feeling that all blessings are descending from above into our hearts and homes, may our grateful love ascend from the altar of our home and heart to thee. We can give thee nothing but our love, — may we give thee this, at least, O our best and dearest Friend. We love thee, because thou hast first loved us; we trust in thee, because thy hand has always led, and is leading us, safely onward and upward. We rise toward thee on the pinions of aspiration and reverence. We submit to thy will as to that which is always wise, right, and good. So may we, this evening, all rest in the quiet sense of thy perfect protection; which we ask in the spirit of Jesus Christ. *Amen.*

XLVIII.

EVIL AND IDLE SPEAKING.

Words are mighty, words are living:
Serpents with their venomous stings,
Or bright angels, crowding round us,
With heaven's light upon their wings!
Every word has its own spirit,
True or false, that never dies;
Every word man's lips have uttered
Echoes in God's skies.
A. A. PROCTER.

Let no corrupt communication proceed out of your mouth, but that which is good to the use of edifying, that it may minister grace unto the hearers.

May I never hear with pleasure, nor ever repeat, such things as dishonor God or injure my neighbor. — *Wilson.*

Set a watch, O Lord, before my mouth, and keep the door of my lips.

Speak not evil one of another.

A froward man soweth strife; and a whisperer separateth chief friends.

Lay not to my charge what, by an angry spirit, by vain and idle words, by foolish jesting, I have committed against thee. — *Wilson.*

Whoso offereth praise glorifieth me: and to him that ordereth his conversation aright will I show the salvation of God.

The mouth of the righteous speaketh wisdom, and his tongue talketh of judgment.

Every beam of reason and ray of knowledge checks the dissolutions of the tongue. — *Taylor.*

By thy words thou shalt be justified, and by thy words thou shalt be condemned.

Keep thy tongue from evil, and thy lips from speaking guile.

Preserve me, O God, from a vain conversation. Give me grace never to be ashamed or afraid to speak to thee, or of thy law. — *Wilson.*

Let your speech be always with grace, seasoned with salt, that ye may know how ye ought to answer every man.

Shun profane and vain babblings; for they will increase unto more ungodliness. And their word will eat as doth a canker.

MORNING.

OUR Father which art in heaven, thou hast set before us again a fresh, new day. The sun rises, the land is full of thy light, and the earth is vocal with thy praises. Birds and beasts, winds and waters, through all ages have lifted up the everlasting song to Him that made them. But far above all the lowest whisper sounds to heaven out of the heart of every man thy child. In the awful power of human speech, faint and broken though it be, thou hast folded more than in all the sounds of

wind and sea. Father, we shall go out into the
world to-day bearing this great gift of the word,
the crown and glory of our life. O help us to
weigh its mighty worth, and to hold it for the ho-
liest uses. May the word we utter this day be a
pure transcript of the truth as we *know* the truth,
whether it bring us loss or gain, sorrow or joy.
Fill us with a great sense and conviction that the
words we speak this day will live to bring their own
harvest of honor or shame, to set the seal of Christ
on our forehead in the last day, or to brand us with
the mark of the beast. Lord, we are in the world,
— keep us, we beseech thee; hold us fast in a true,
sweet temper to all men, in a strong, clear sense of
our real duty; save us from harsh words, from
petty words, from unfair and from foolish words,
and may we be so full of thy good spirit, so open
and free, that some man or woman, sad and weary
from the burdens and sorrows of life, may gather
new power out of some word of cheer that may
fall from our lips, and be able to cry, " Did not our
hearts burn within. us as he talked to us by the
way?" This in the spirit of Jesus Christ. *Amen.*

EVENING.

WE pray, Heavenly Parent, for wisdom to
form our characters after the pattern of our
Master, and to guide our lives according to the

lines of thy law. We pray to thee for help to
order our thoughts in accordance with truth, and to
frame our speech to issues of purity and good.
May no word of falsehood or hatred drop from our
tongues, but abundant words of wisdom and kindness, sound admonition and blessed encouragement.
Make us slow to blame, quick to praise, even as
we would have others be to us. Lead us also to
cultivate the listening ear and the improving heart,
that no words of usefulness from our fellow-men,
or from thy providence, may pass us unheeded.
Speak unto us ever, O God, the counsels we need,
and give us the will to obey. We would remember
that we must give an account of every idle word,
and be inspired by the thought to live with a dis-
creet oversight of ourselves, purifying the heart,
curbing the tongue, aiming at thine approval here
and thine acceptance hereafter. *Amen.*

XLIX.

REPENTANCE AND FORGIVENESS.

Times without number have I prayed,
" This only once forgive,"
Relapsing when thy hand was stayed,
And suffered me to live.

Yet now the kingdom of thy peace,
Lord, to my heart restore;
Forgive my vain repentances,
And bid me sin no more.

COWPER.

If the wicked will turn from all his sins that he hath committed, and keep all my statutes, and do that which is lawful and right, he shall surely live.

Have mercy upon me, O God, according to thy lovingkindness: according unto the multitude of thy tender mercies blot out my transgressions.

Wash me thoroughly from mine iniquity, and cleanse me from my sin.

Turn us unto thee, O Lord, and we shall be turned; renew our days as of old.

Remember, O Lord, thy tender mercies and thy lovingkindnesses; for they have been ever of old.

Repentance begins in the humiliation of the heart, and ends in the reformation of the life. — *Mason.*

Let the wicked forsake his way, and the unrighteous man

9 *

his thoughts; and let him return unto the Lord, and he will have mercy upon him; and to our God, for he will abundantly pardon.

As I live, saith the Lord God, I have no pleasure in the death of the wicked; but that the wicked turn from his way and live.

Remember not the sins of my youth, nor my transgressions.

The Lord is nigh unto them that are of a broken heart; and saveth such as be of a contrite spirit.

Bitter in their bud, fruits gain sweetness as they advance to their maturity; so it is with the exercises of penitence, — they begin by being bitter, but they end by growing sweet. — *St. Ephraim.*

Though your sins be as scarlet, saith the Lord, they shall be white as snow; though they be red like crimson, they shall be as wool.

Repentance is the key that unlocks the gate wherein sin keeps man a prisoner. — *Feltham.*

MORNING.

FATHER and Friend, thou who art all holy and pure, burdened with a sense of sin and a weight of transgression, weighed down by a heavy heart, all-conscious of its evil, we come to thee. We come, though we are sinners, — yes, we come because we are sinners. There is no better reason, thou hast taught us in Christ, for coming to thee, than we have in our sin. If we were pure and righteous, we should not need thy pardoning love;

but because we are sinful, we need it; and because thou knowest that we need it, thou art sending it. O Thou, who art in Christ reconciling sinners to thyself, reconcile us to thyself. Change this death into life; let the burden drop from us; lift us out of this mire and deep water, in which we can neither stand nor go, — lift us, and put our feet upon the rock which shall never be moved. Let thy forgiveness teach us to love; because thou forgivest much, may we love much, in return. Looking behind us, we see our lives imperfect, our souls stained, our best works poor, our plainest duties unfulfilled. How much time have we wasted, how many opportunities have we lost. In thought and affection, in word and deed, against each other and against thee, how much have we done wrong, and omitted to do of right. Looking around us, we see so much that we ought to do, and are doing so little, so many who need, and we so poor and negligent to give. Looking within us, how little we find of faith, love, and peace. Dark, stormy, and wild are our thoughts and feelings, too often, — how seldom filled with the sense of thy mercies and love. Looking before us, what can we hope? We can hope nothing away from thee, or without thee. In thee alone, God of our life, is our hope. In thee alone, through thy Son our Saviour. In thee alone, through the power of redemption and pardon in him. In thee, in thee, Infinite Love, abyss of mercy, ever-flowing Fountain, inexhaustible in grace, — in thee we will trust, hope, and have rest. Help us to trust and be forgiven, to trust and be saved, to trust now and forever. *Amen.*

EVENING.

FATHER of an infinite majesty! Father of mercies unceasing and unalterable! Laden with another day's experience of thy goodness, we gather ourselves around thy mercy-seat. As this lower world sinks into the shadow, and the upper world of light unfolds itself, and we see the hand of power and wisdom revealed in the wonders above us, and feel the hand of a tender providence drawing the curtain of the night around us, and laid upon our heads in benediction, O our holy Father, the sense of thy greatness and of thy goodness fills our souls at once with gratitude and with sorrow. We feel how poorly we have prized and used the opportunities of good which thou hast this day lent us, how often we have sent back thine angels and grieved away thy Holy Spirit, how often we have suffered the vanities of this world to hide from us the beauty of holiness, and the vexations of life to drown the voice of wisdom in our hearts.

But, O long-suffering and tenderly faithful Parent, we feel in the hush of this evening hour the voice of Jesus whispering of One who is not willing that any child of his should perish. By thy restraining grace, not yet has the false light of evil passion nor the dismal shadow of unbelief quite hid from us the glories of thy kingdom. O may thy goodness lead us to repentance. Breathe thy peace into our hearts. Gather us under the shadow of thy everlasting wings, and may this eventide be light round about us, and grant us a sweet foretaste of that rest which remaineth for the people of God. *Amen.*

L.

INWARD PEACE.

We ask for peace, O Lord!
Thy children ask thy peace;
Not what the world calls rest,
That toil and care should cease.

. . . . .

We ask THY *peace, O Lord!*
Through storm, and fear, and strife,
To light and guide us on
Through a long struggling life.

A. A. PROCTER.

O, how great peace and quietness should he possess, that would cut off all vain anxiety, and think only upon divine things, and such as are profitable for his soul, and would place all his confidence in God. — *À Kempis.*

Mark the perfect man, and behold the upright, for the end of that man is peace.

Peace does not dwell in outward things, but within the soul. We may preserve it in the midst of the bitterest pain, if our will remain firm and submissive.

Peace in this life springs from acquiescence even in disagreeable things, not in an exemption from suffering. — *Fénelon.*

Great peace have they which love thy law; and nothing shall offend them.

Put on charity, which is the bond of perfectness, and let the peace of God rule in your hearts.

Resign every forbidden joy; restrain every wish that is not referred to His will; banish all eager desires, all anxiety. Desire only the will of God; seek him alone, and you will find peace; you shall enjoy it in spite of the world. — *Fénelon.*

The peace of God, which passeth all understanding, shall keep your hearts and minds through Christ Jesus.

The work of righteousness shall be peace; and the effect of righteousness, quietness and assurance forever.

There is no peace, saith my God, to the wicked.

The fruit of righteousness is sown in peace of them that make peace.

Thou wilt keep him in perfect peace whose mind is stayed on thee; because he trusteth in thee.

When he giveth quietness, who then can make trouble?

MORNING.

FATHER in heaven, whom thine own heaven of blessedness cannot remove from us thine earthly creatures, we beseech thee to grant unto us the peace that this world cannot bestow. We marvel sometimes that we are so much troubled, that clouds gather over our fortunes, anxieties invade our hearts, and bereavements darken our homes. We will not deny that there is to us frequent mystery in thy dealings with us. Yet we bless thee, O God, that thy way is justified every day more and more by the hand of thy providence, and light riseth in the midst of darkness to us according as we keep thy law and trust in thy love.

We rejoice that thou hast taught us that there is more good in store for us than what the world calls pleasure, happiness, and success. We bless thee, that, through trial and disappointment and mortification, we are led to seek abiding peace, and through the cross of suffering we may win the crown of joy. We give thee thanks for thy comforting spirit in the former seasons of our own darkness, and beseech thee to sustain and guide us in all time to come.

Enable us, Almighty and All-Merciful, so to control and school our senses as to keep us from inflaming passions and debasing indulgences. Help us so to order our lives as to meet our cares by due method, and do our work and bear our burdens without indolence or distraction. In all our relations with kindred, friends, and the world, may we have a kindly and earnest and even temper, so as to walk in the love that thinketh no evil and believest in all good.

And, O our Father, more than for any earthly gift or human solace, we pray for the presence and help of thy Holy Spirit, the Heavenly Comforter, that we may have the indwelling peace of filial faith and obedience and communion that is the blessed life of the children of God. Graciously hear us, through Jesus Christ our Lord. *Amen.*

EVENING.

DEAR Father in Heaven! Thy strong and gentle hand hath led us during another of thy days, and our hearts are drawn to thee in thankful acknowledgments of thy sweet grace. Bless the Lord, O our souls! How thy mercies have been multiplied upon us, as we have gone about in thy strength, and under thy large and loving providence, and with endeavors to obey thee, to serve our brethren and friends, and to do the nearest duty. O Lord, we know that every labor of love, even the least, is remembered by thee ; and if we have been permitted this day to do the humblest work in the spirit of our dear Lord and Saviour, we bless thee, our soul's Light and Life, we thank thee that we have been suffered to share in any measure with Him who hath redeemed us, and is calling us with a heavenly calling. Help us to live nearer to thee, and in a better obedience. If at any time we have failed to heed thy summons, and have gone away to please ourselves, may we heartily repent, and be found henceforth in thy vineyard, laboring in his service, and for the love of him who said, " My Father worketh hitherto, and I work." May our light so shine before men, that they, seeing our good works, may glorify thee, and follow us in our following of Christ. In all humility, and deeply sensible of our unworthiness, we do pray that we may show forth and complete our faith by our works. O God, let us never forget that the night cometh in which no man can work. Guardian of our bodies and of our souls, we commend ourselves to thy watchful care during the hours of darkness and of slumber. Thou sendest sleep to thy beloved, that they may serve thee the better when the sun shall again shine upon our pathways. May we rest, only that we may the more earnestly labor. In the arms of thy dear Christ may the souls of our loved ones repose. Shield them from all harm, even from the very thought of evil, and when days and nights shall all be ended, pour upon us of the light of that sun which shall never more go down, and may he who is in the midst of the throne evermore lead us and feed us, and unto thy great name, O thou Father of the Christ, shall be the glory. *Amen.*

LI.

TRUST IN GOD.

The God of love my shepherd is,
And he that doth me feed:
While he is mine, and I am his,
What can I want or need?
HERBERT.

Put thy trust in God; let him be thy fear and thy love he shall answer for thee, and will do in all things what is best for thee. — *À Kempis.*

It is better to put trust in God than to put confidence in man.

Some trust in chariots, and some in horses; but we will remember the name of the Lord our God.

Trust not in uncertain riches, but in the living God, who giveth us richly all things to enjoy.

Let us set no bounds to our confidence in God. Let us repress all eagerness, all inquietude. He who trusts in God becomes immovable as Mount Zion. — *Fénelon.*

In thee, therefore, O Lord God, I place my whole hope and refuge; on thee I rest all my tribulation and anguish; for I find all to be weak and inconstant, whatsoever I behold out of thee. — *À Kempis.*

For many friends cannot profit, nor strong helpers assist, nor prudent counsellors give a profitable answer, nor the books of the learned afforded comfort, nor any precious substance deliver, nor any place, however retired and lovely, give shelter, unless thou dost assist, help, strengthen, console, instruct, and guard us. — *À Kempis.*

Without God, our existence has no support, our life no aim, our improvements no permanence, our best labors no sure and enduring results. — *Channing.*

Trust in the Lord, and do good; so shalt thou dwell in the land, and verily thou shalt be fed.

How excellent is thy loving-kindness, O God! therefore the children of men put their trust under the shadow of thy wings.

Blessed is the man that trusteth in the Lord, and whose hope the Lord is.

For he shall be as a tree planted by the waters.

The Lord redeemeth the soul of his servants; and none of them that trust in him shall be desolate.

Trust in the Lord forever; for the Lord Jehovah is everlasting strength.

Wait on the Lord; be of good courage, and he shall strengthen thine heart.

MORNING.

O THOU most holy and ever-loving God, we thank thee once more for the quiet rest of the night that has gone by, for the new promise that has come with this fresh morning, and for the hope of this day. While we have slept, the world in which we live has swept on in its awful space, great fires have burned under us, great waters have been all about us, and great storms above us; but thou hast held them back by thy strong hand, and we have rested under the shadow of thy love. The bird sat on the spray out in the darkness, the flower nestled in the grass, we lay down in our home, and all slept in the arms of God. The bird will trust thee this day to give its morsel of meat, and the flower will trust thee for its fresh raiment; so may we trust thee this day for all the needs of the body, the soul, and the spirit. Give us this day our daily bread. O Father, this day may bring some hard task to our life, or some hard trial to our love. We may grow weary, or sad, or hopeless in our lot. But, Father, our whole life until now has been one great proof of thy care. Bread has come for our body, thoughts to our mind, love to our heart, and all from thee. So help us, we implore thee, while we stand still on this side of all that the day may bring, and while we are strong and quiet from the baptism of the night, to resolve that we will trust thee this day to shine into any gloom of the mind, to stand by us in any trial of our love, and to give us rest in thy good time as we need.

May this day be full of a power that shall bring us near to thee, and make us more like thee; and, O God, may we so trust thee this day, that when the day is done our trust shall be firmer than ever. Then when our last day comes, and our work is done, may we trust thee in death and forever, in the spirit of Jesus Christ our Lord. *Amen.*

EVENING.

O GLORIOUS and ever-blessed God, — whose word called all things into being, by whom all things exist, whose attributes are beyond all our powers of thought, — how should we dare in our ignorance and our weakness to call upon thee, how dare hope that thou wouldst regard our prayer, hadst thou not thyself called us thy children, and bidden us come unto thee as unto a father. Pour out upon us now, we beseech thee, the spirit of adoption, that we may truly and earnestly repent of our past ingratitude to thee, and of all our sins against each other, and against any of our fellow-men; and that we may lie down to rest in the calm assurance that our sins are forgiven, that we have been accepted in the Beloved, and that we have been born again, — born of God, adopted by thee into the new household which is named of Christ.

O Lord, we confess the boldness of our prayers, but we know that perfect love casteth out fear, and we pray that we may be perfected in love. We know that we are not worthy to ask aught of thee, but we also rejoice to know that thou art ever ready to give good gifts to those who ask in penitence and faith; and that thou wilt cause all things to work together for good to them that love thee.

Overshadow us, O Father, and all for whom we

in our hearts would pray, continually with thy loving presence. Let there be no night in our hearts, but may we ever have the light of thy countenance shining upon us. Make us strong to rejoice in doing or in bearing whatsoever thou mayst require of us, and grant that, when the evening of life comes to us, we may each one, surely trusting in thy love, lie down in hope of awaking transformed in the glorious image of Him through whom we would offer every prayer. *Amen.*

LII.

A CONSCIENCE VOID OF OFFENCE.

Quick as the apple of an eye,
O God! my conscience make;
Awake my soul when sin is nigh,
And keep it still awake.
C. WESLEY.

The glory of the good is in their consciences, and not in the tongues of men. The gladness of the just is of God, and in God; and their joy is of the truth. — *À Kempis.*

When the Gentiles, which have not the law, do by nature the things contained in the law, these having not the law, are a law unto themselves.

Which show the work of the law written in their hearts,

their conscience also bearing witness, and their thoughts the meanwhile accusing or else excusing one another.

That the eye of conscience may be always quick and lively, let constant use be sure to keep it constantly open, and thereby ready and prepared to admit and let in those heavenly beams which are always streaming forth from God upon minds fitted to receive them. — *South.*

Now the end of the commandment is charity out of a pure heart, and of a good conscience, and of faith unfeigned.

Bless me in this life with but peace of my conscience, command of my affections, the love of thyself and my dearest friends, and I shall be happy. — *Sir Thomas Browne.*

Our rejoicing is this, the testimony of our conscience, that in simplicity and godly sincerity, not with fleshly wisdom, but by the grace of God, we have had our conversation in this world.

If our heart condemn us not, then have we confidence towards God.

Let me rather choose to die, than to sin against my conscience. — *Wilson.*

Morning.

INFINITE and holy God, in this morning light we would come to thee with our offering of grateful worship. Whom have we in heaven but thee ; and there is none upon earth that we can desire in comparison with thee. We thank thee, Heavenly Father, for this new day, the gift of thy love, the accepted time, the day of salvation. Our duties wait for us ; the work given us to do requires all our strength. Father, help us to work in such a spirit of devotedness and trust, with such singleness of purpose, that our life may all be in harmony with thy mighty agencies. May we work in such wisdom, and with such reference to thy will, that what we seek we shall find. A pure and unsullied conscience, may we possess it ; the Christ-like spirit, may it be our inspiration. To-day may we have faith to commit ourselves to Christian principles, and follow the Master. Though appetite and sense should crave indulgence ; though the world should tempt, or frown and threaten ; though doubts and fears should rise up against us ; may we dare to do right, and be strong to rise above sin. O, to-day may we have Jesus at our side, as a mighty brother to counsel us, and with deep spiritual sympathies to uplift us. With our hand in his, we cannot go astray ; with our eye upon the beauty of his holiness, we cannot fail to hunger and thirst after righteousness.

O God, chasten and sanctify the eager, anxious thoughts and desires of the business world ; may all learn what it means to seek first the kingdom of God and his righteousness, trusting that all these things shall be added. Help us to make thy will our rule of duty, to be fellow-laborers with thee, and so to have Omnipotence for our stay and support. O save us from temptations that might overpower us. Lead us in the way we should go.

Father of forgiving mercy, save us from our sins, and strengthen us to be pure and noble and holy, like thy Son. As his disciples, we wait for thy blessing, and render to thee praise and thanksgiving for ever and ever. *Amen.*

EVENING.

INFINITE Being of justice and truth, who holdest nations and men fast bound by thine eternal law, amid the solemn stillness of night we humbly bow in confession of thy majesty and our dependence, of thy goodness and our unworthiness. As the shadows gather about us, we would commune with thee, and be still. Beneath thine all-seeing eye, who knowest us better than we know ourselves, we would examine our souls. Search thou our hearts and try our thoughts; see if there be any wicked way in us, and lead us in the way everlasting.

We thank thee for that departing light which has made the world glorious to our sight this day, revealing the tokens of thy love on every hand. Still more we praise thee for that inner light which lightens every man that cometh into the world, which shines in immortal glory from saintly souls, illumining the path of the divine life, and revealing the riches of the spiritual world. Quicken thou our inward vision. Give us the purity of heart that shall see thee. By faith may we behold the eternal realities for which we should live and labor. By the teaching of thy word, by the spirit of Christ, and by daily experience may our conscience be trained clearly to discern through all perplexities the way of duty. Grant us quick moral sense to detect and repel all lurking sin, and to discover and obey the right. May no delusion of outward sense betray us to put error for truth or choose evil for good.

Every day teaches us that we are not sufficient unto ourselves. Following our own desires too readily, we stray from the strait path that leadeth unto life. Trusting on our own strength, we falter and fail. Only in thy light can we see light. In thee only is our strength and safety. Accept and bless the humble efforts to serve thee which this day has witnessed. Pity our frailties and forgive our sins. May past success encourage us to renewed endeavor; may past failure admonish us to cleave more closely to the strictest rule of right. In future peril be thou, O God, our safeguard and shield. Keep our feet far from the paths that lead to destruction. Make us superior to temptation. Through all coming days may we maintain consciences void of offence toward thee and our fellow-man. Let the setting sun find no anger or alienation in our hearts toward any brother. Forgiving, as we hope to be forgiven; forbearing one another's faults, since none is perfect, may we, as far as consistent with purity and truth, live peaceably with all men. Offending none by thought, word, or deed, reconciled to all, proving by brotherly love our love toward thee, let the incense of our grateful and obedient hearts rise to thy throne and bring all needed blessing down. We commit ourselves and commend our brethren to thy fatherly providence. Refresh us for the duties which another day shall bring. Prepare us for the everlasting morning, where, in higher service, we may live to thy glory. *Amen.*

LIII.

GIVEN TO HOSPITALITY.

By Thy pitying spirit guided,
Jesus sought the sufferer's door;
Comfort for the poor provided
And the mourner's sorrows bore.

Father, as thy love is endless,
Working by thy servants thus,
The forsaken and the friendless
Deign to visit, e'en by us.

PIERPONT.

Use hospitality one to another without grudging.

When thou makest a dinner or a supper, call not thy friends, nor thy brethren, neither thy kinsmen, nor thy rich neighbors; lest they also bid thee again, and a recompense be made thee.

But when thou makest a feast, call the poor, the maimed, the lame, the blind,

And thou shalt be blessed; for they cannot recompense thee; for thou shalt be recompensed at the resurrection of the just.

Blessed is he that considereth the poor: the Lord will deliver him in time of trouble.

Be not forgetful to entertain strangers: for thereby some have entertained angels unawares.

Exercise the duties of hospitality, kindly and continually; not receiving strangers with that cold and ceremonious politeness which exists only upon the lips, but affectionately. — *St. Jerome.*

When thou seest misery in thy brother's face, let him see mercy in thine eye: the more the oil of mercy is poured on him by thy pity, the more the oil in thy cruse shall be increased. — *Quarles.*

Mercy is more acceptable to God, than all sacrifices. — *St. Chrysostom.*

If thine enemy hunger, feed him; if he thirst, give him drink; for in so doing thou shalt heap coals of fire on his head.

MORNING.

GIVER of all good, and Fountain of all joy, what rich feasts for our senses and our souls does thy fatherly love offer anew with each returning morning. How hast thou filled the earth with bounty and adorned it with beauty for our benefit. We see thy mercy freshly revealed in the light and privilege of this new day. Again we hear thy gracious invitations to come up higher and enjoy the felicity of heavenly things.

Thanks we give thee for the returning light and our daily bread; for home and health and friends; for the instructions of thy truth and the opportunities of thy service; for repeated warnings against sin, and the ample rewards that crown our fidelity; for the sweet and kindly ties that bind us one to another, and the pure affections that spring up in our hearts, fountains of bliss unspeakable; for all that renders this world a pleasant home, and fits us for the life to come.

Teach us, O Father, to imitate thine own boundless beneficence. Freely as we have received, so freely may we give. We would not selfishly appropriate thy favor, but would know the deeper bliss of ministering to others' needs. Quicken within us the fountains of generosity; warm our sympathies toward the sufferer of every class and clime; let no unbrotherly prejudice ever close our homes or hearts against any child of thine. May our faith in Christ be no empty profession, but lead us to honor him in the persons of the sick, the imprisoned, the unfortunate, — his brethren and ours. Following in the footsteps of his self-denial and brotherly service, may we become the almoners of thy bounty and saviours of souls.

When Truth knocks at the door of our hearts, may no indifference or prejudice forbid its entrance, but as an angel visitant may it find hospitable welcome. Gladly would we hail every message from heaven, however severe the toil or costly the sacrifice to which it calls us. To thy messengers, whether of joy or grief, of life or death, we would lend attentive ear. And to the heavenly visions thou showest us may we never prove disobedient.

Father, forgive us as we forgive those who wrong us. Keep us this day without sin, and may its passing hours render us more worthy of thy love. Let thy kind providence extend to those near and dear to us, and to all for whom we should pray. And may the time speedily come when thy glory shall fill the world as the waters fill the sea. *Amen.*

EVENING.

O GOD, we gather and bend before thee again in this good home, where we dwell in peace and in plenty. The power to make this home is from thee; the power to sustain it is from thee. Thou hast made us to differ from the homeless by thy pure mercy; by thy will our life is strong; by thy will we fade away into bare need, and cry to thee for bread. Father, hast thou not made us to differ that we may give unto others as thou hast given unto us ? Deepen, we beseech thee, our sense of thy great bounty; help us to see why we are so blessed. May we know that these good things are given for great and generous uses. The poor we have always with us; the stranger comes to our door; friends dwell near us whose life will be more cheerful if they may freely enter with us into this cheerful place. O grant that thy spirit may touch us, so that we may gladly give of our bread to them that hunger, and our shelter to the Son of Man who has not where to lay his head. May we know that in all guises thine angels come to us, and grow radiant only after they are gone. And may we make the presence of our home felt all about us, in this place where we dwell; may no sect or party name ever close our hearts and our home to the good, of *any* name or nation. So may these fruits of good living in all pureness make this dwelling to all what thou hast made it to us, as the house of God and the very gate of heaven. Then, being faithful in our few things, may we know that thou hast said, " Well done," and enter into thy joy, through Jesus Christ. *Amen.*

LIV.

CONFORMITY TO THE WILL OF GOD.

The best will is our Father's will,
And we may rest there calm and still;
O, make it hour by hour thine own,
And wish for naught but that alone
Which pleaseth God.

PAUL GERHARDT.

Christ said, Whosoever shall do the will of God, the same is my brother, and my sister and mother.

Teach me, O Lord, to do thy will; teach me to live worthily and humbly in thy sight; for thou art my wisdom, thou dost truly know me. — *À Kempis.*

Let us desire that God's will be done, and only his, and we shall make a heaven of earth. — *Fénelon.*

All men are members of one body, and, in order to be happy, it is necessary they should conform their own private wills to that universal will which governs the whole body. — *Pascal.*

For this is the will of God, even your sanctification.

May we no longer follow our own inclinations, but may we not only pray, and teach, and suffer, but eat, drink, and converse, — do all things, with reference to his will. — *Fénelon.*

Not with eye-service as men-pleasers; but as the servants of Christ, doing the will of God from the heart.

For in truth, the reason why sin is sin, is merely because it is contrary to the will of God. If, therefore, when he discovers his will to us by events, we sin if we do not conform ourselves to it. — *Pascal.*

Be not conformed to this world; but be ye transformed by the renewing of your mind, that ye may prove what is that good and acceptable and perfect will of God.

It is better, if the will of God be so, that ye suffer for well-doing than for evil-doing.

Teach me to do thy will; for thou art my God: thy Spirit is good; lead me into the land of uprightness.

MORNING.

O THOU whose sleepless providence shelters and sustains us through darkness and danger, with the opening morning we lift our hearts to thee in gratitude and trust. To thy service we would dedicate our time and talents, asking renewed light and strength for all our needs. Father, fill us with thine own spirit of justice, mercy, and truth. May thy will be ours in duty and in trial, and in acquaintance with thee let our souls find peace.

Borne up in the arms of thy loving-kindness, never forgotten, but cared for with more than an earthly parent's love, we would look to thee in filial confidence, believing that thou knowest what is best for us, and that thou doest all things well. Teach us that when we disobey thee we wrong our own souls; while, to those who faithfully serve thee, thou bringest better results than we can foresee or

10 *   o

plan. Profoundly impress it upon our hearts, that our only real enemy is sin, that naught can harm us but our own wrong-doing, that all things work for good to those who love God.

As we go forth this day, may a lively sense of duty so penetrate and sanctify our humblest labors, that, whether we eat or drink, or whatever we do, we shall live to thy glory. To the great principles of right illustrated in Jesus may we unreservedly commit ourselves, and follow without faltering wherever they shall show the way. And though they summon us to surrender our dearest interests, may we willingly give up all outward good for the richer satisfactions to which they surely lead.

In trial or grief we would cheerfully accept whatever lot thou shalt ordain. Do with us as thou wilt, O Lord. Drawing nigh to Jesus by faith, may his fidelity and submission inspire us to go forth upon our Father's work, and, when the bitter cup is offered, to say, " Father, thy will, not mine, be done." And whether called to part with earthly treasure, or friends dear to our hearts, still may we say, " The Lord gave, and the Lord hath taken away. Blessed be the name of the Lord."

Father, forgive our sins and shortcomings, and grant those things thou seest we need. Hallowed be thy name. Thy kingdom come, thy will be done on earth as in heaven. Thine is the kingdom, the power, and the glory, forever. *Amen.*

EVENING.

O GOD, our Heavenly Father, have mercy upon us. Thou knowest our hearts, and how sorely we are tried. Have pity upon us, and bring us into a perfect submission to thy will. Help us always to accept thy will as the highest end and law of life. If flesh and heart are weak, be thou our strength and our portion. Grant to us our daily bread ; grant health, and strength, and friends, and all the earthly comforts that we need. But if, in thy richer mercy and thy more comprehensive love, thou seest fit to withdraw thine earthly gifts, — even those most dear and precious to us, — help us to bear the loss with patient and thankful submission. Thou, O God, didst give, and thou dost take away, blessed be thy name. Only draw us more closely to thy bosom. Breathe into us the spirit of thy Son, through which we also may be lifted above our earthly griefs, and, in our sorest privations and afflictions, each one of us may say, I thank thee, O Father, Lord of heaven and earth ; even so, Father, for so it seemed good in thy sight. So may each earthly loss become to us a heavenly gain. So may every new trial, through thy grace, which is sufficient for us, refine and purify our hearts, bring us into closer sympathy with thee, and, transforming us more and more into the image of our Lord, prepare us for that

world where there shall be no more sorrow nor
crying, neither any more pain, and where God
shall wipe away all tears from our eyes, through
Jesus Christ our Lord. *Amen.*

L V.

HELP THOU OUR UNBELIEF.

Father! when o'er our trembling hearts
   Doubt's shadows gathering brood,
When faith in thee almost departs,
   And gloomiest fears intrude;
Forsake us not, O God of grace,
   But send those fears relief;
Grant us again to see thy face;
   Lord, help our unbelief.
                  BULFINCH.

Jesus saith unto them, Have faith in God.

Take heed, lest there be in any of you an evil heart of
unbelief, in departing from the living God.

For the gospel of Christ is the power of God unto salvation
to every one that believeth: to the Jew first, and also to the
Greek.

For therein is the righteousness of God revealed from faith
to faith: as it is written, The just shall live by faith.

Faith must lay our hearts to rest in the will of God, amid
all the changes of life and death. — *Baxter.*

I say unto you, What things soever ye desire when ye pray, believe that ye receive them, and ye shall have them.

But without faith it is impossible to please God; for he that cometh to him must believe that he is, and that he is a rewarder of them that diligently seek him.

Jesus saith, According to your faith be it unto you.

Trust in the Living God who is the Saviour of all men, specially of those who believe.

Verily I say unto you, If ye have faith as a grain of mustard-seed, ye shall say unto this mountain, Remove hence to yonder place, and it shall remove; and nothing shall be impossible unto you.

In Jesus Christ neither circumcision availeth anything, nor uncircumcision; but faith which worketh by love.

Lord, increase our faith.

Jesus said, If thou canst believe, all things are possible to him that believeth.

Lord, I believe; help thou mine unbelief.

MORNING.

ALMIGHTY God, by whose goodness we again behold the morning light, we desire to begin this day with thee. By looking up unto thee in thankful trust, we would assure our souls of thy nearness to us, and renew the joy and peace of believing. Amid all the scenes through which we are called to pass this day, let our minds rest trustingly and peacefully in thee. For every labor and duty may we receive needed strength from on high. Suffer us not to be led into any new temptation, nor be overcome by easily besetting sins. Let no pleasures beguile us into forgetfulness of thee. Let no disappointments cause us for a moment to distrust thy fatherly goodness. Let no irritations provoke us to anger or to fretfulness; and though clouds should gather in our sky, may there be a clear shining of thy light within us. As thou art to be seen in the face of Jesus Christ, yearning with pity and love to the children of men, so may we ever behold thee; and may this blessed manifestation of thy tender compassions awaken in each of our bosoms continual responses of gratitude, submission, and obedience. May no events ever shake our faith in thee, but may our daily experience confirm and establish it more and more. May our walk with thee be so close, that in every step of life we shall feel that thy hand is leading us. Go with us, we beseech thee, through the hours of this day, defending us from the evil; and so rule in our hearts by thy spirit, that, at their close, we may have the testimony of our consciences that we have failed in no duty, and have kept ourselves unspotted from the world.

Unite us all to one another in the closest bonds of purity and affection; and may our kindred and friends, wherever their lot is cast, be joint partakers with us in the blessings of thy providence and the

riches of thy grace. Hear us, O God, we humbly
beseech thee, in these desires and petitions of our
hearts, and accept the homage of our unfeigned
gratitude, love, and praise, through Jesus Christ
our Lord. *Amen.*

EVENING.

O THOU whose gracious power has this day
defended us from evil, and whose precious
promise is that thou wilt be the God of those who
shall be thy people, make us to be numbered with
thy saints, and grant that we may ever be under
the guidance of thy Spirit, as we are under the care
of thy providence. We thank thee for all the mercies that thou hast bestowed upon us hitherto, and
acknowledge that we have not returned unto thee
the thanksgiving of obedience as we ought. O
Father, let us now feel the fulfilment of the
prophet's word, that at evening time it shall be light;
and may the clouds that have arisen and hidden
thy throne from us now pass away. Sanctify our
hearts, and make us so pure that we may see thee,
and see all things transfigured in the glorious light
of thy presence. Let the unseen things of faith
become to us, as they are in truth, things real and
eternal; and let the things of time and sense be to
us, as they in truth are, unsubstantial and transient.
Whensoever, O gracious Father, our eyes become

dim, our faith feeble, and our love cold, then send'
into our hearts that holy influence which shall bring
to our minds the words of Christ, — the eternal
words which shall endure when heaven and earth
have passed away, and let those words be the rock
on which we build, whence we may see, with un-
clouded eyes, the heavenly land; let those words fill
us with that love and peace and charity which is
our foretaste of the heaven to come.

Bless us, O God, and all those for whom we
would pray, with these gifts of thy grace; let thy
kingdom come in all the earth; let thy will be done
here below as in heaven above. For thine is the
kingdom and the power; thine be, through Christ
our Lord, the glory evermore. *Amen.*

LVI.

CONSIDER YOUR WAYS.

Thus far on life's perplexing path,
  Thus far the Lord our steps hath led;
Safe from the world's pursuing wrath,
  Unharmed though floods hung o'er our head;
Here then we pause, look back, adore,
  Like ransomed Israel from the shore.

MONTGOMERY.

Now, therefore, thus saith the Lord of hosts, Consider your
ways.

I said, l will take heed to my ways, that I sin not with my tongue.

Ponder the path of thy feet, and let all thy ways be established.

There is a way which seemeth right unto a man, but the ends thereof are the ways of death.

O that my ways were directed to keep thy statutes!

Let us search and try our ways, and turn again to the Lord.

Blessed are the undefiled in the way, who walk in the law of the Lord.

Let us remember our way, and where we are, and keep our garments girt up; for we walk amidst thorns and briers, which, if we let them down, will entangle and stop us, and possibly tear our garments. — *Leighton.*

Enter not into the path of the wicked, and go not in the way of evil men.

Avoid it, pass not by it, turn from it, and pass away.

Trust in the Lord with all thy heart. In all thy ways acknowledge him, and he shall direct thy paths.

Hold up my goings in thy paths, that my footsteps slip not.

Thou compassest my path and my lying down, and art acquainted with all my ways.

Search me, O God, and know mine heart; try me, and know my thoughts ;

And see if there be any wicked way in me, and lead me in the way everlasting.

MORNING.

ALMIGHTY God, by whose gracious ordinance man goeth forth to his work and his

labor until the evening, assist us, we humbly beseech thee, before we engage in the duties and
labors of this day, to call to remembrance the benefits we have received at thy hand in days past, to
ponder the paths our feet have trodden, and to consider our thoughts and our ways, whether they
have been ordered according to thy word. Expose
unto us, O God, the things that are hidden in our
hearts, that we, seeing our guilt, may bring unto
thee the sacrifice of a humble and contrite spirit,
and by the prevalency of our prayers may obtain
grace to help in every future time of need. Enable
us to search ourselves, as in thy sight, and from
all the evil of our wicked desires and unrighteous
doings, good Lord deliver us. Let not our transgressions be brought into judgment against us, nor
separate us from thy love in Christ Jesus our Lord.
Kindle our hearts to thankfulness and our lips to
praise in the remembrance of thy mercies; and let
thy long-suffering to us-ward, while it shows to us
that thou art slow to anger and abundant in goodness, make us heartily ashamed to abuse thy patience by more disobedience. O Thou who seest
our every act and thought, let thine eye be upon
us; and wilt thou direct our steps this day? Let us
not wander into by and forbidden paths, but keep
in the straight and narrow way which leadeth to
thee. Thus may each day bring us one day's
journey nearer to heaven. So may evening and

morning, as in turn they manifest thy goodness and declare thy glory, lead us wisely to consider our way before thee, and devoutly to show forth thy praise. Now unto the King eternal, immortal, invisible, the only wise God, be honor and glory, through Jesus Christ, for ever and ever. *Amen.*

EVENING.

AGAIN, O God, thy mercy has brought us to the close of day. Softly thou hast drawn around us the folds of night, and dost permit us to look for its welcome repose. Yet, O our Father, we would not thoughtlessly resign the hours of this day, but would look back upon them in solemn and reverent thought. Another period of deep responsibility and of precious opportunities has gone, never to return. Another portion of life's great tablet has been written through, and its abiding record is with thee. In thy sacred presence, we would dwell upon the lesson it has taught. Thou knowest whether we have improved the opportunities which it brought, whether we have performed its duties and accepted its discipline aright. Infinite and Holy One, we seek shelter under the wings of thy compassion, as we recall our manifold neglects. Our own hearts condemn us for our ingratitude and sin. And thou art greater than our hearts, and knowest all things. Lord, be merciful to us,

and may the consciousness of thy overflowing goodness, daily and hourly renewed, quicken our love
for thee, and animate us with new desires to do thy
will. Help us, O God, to feel the solemn mystery
of life. Give us a new sense of our infinite capacities and our eternal hopes. Give us new confidence in prayer, increased faith in the divine mission of Jesus, and more fixed and solemn purposes
of duty. And grant that thus we shall not be
homeless and aimless wanderers upon the earth,
but may have ever the rod and staff of a guiding
and sustaining faith. And now unto thee, our kind
Guardian and Defence, we commend ourselves
anew. Keep us, if it be thy will, to see another
day. And grant that the life we shall henceforth
live in the flesh, we may live in the faith and love
of Jesus Christ our Lord. *Amen.*

LVII.

HIS COMPASSIONS FAIL NOT

Fountain of light, and living breath,
Whose mercies never fail nor fade,
Fill me with life that hath no death,
Fill me with light that hath no shade;
Appoint the remnant of my days
To see thy power and sing thy praise.

JOHN QUARLES.

It is of the Lord's mercies that we are not consumed, because his compassions fail not.

They are new every morning : great is thy faithfulness.

Though he cause grief, yet will he have compassion according to the multitude of his mercies.

The Lord is not slack concerning his promise ; but is long-suffering to us-ward, not willing that any should perish, but that all should come to repentance.

Behold, the Lord's hand is not shortened, that it cannot save ; neither his ear heavy, that it cannot hear.

The Lord is slow to anger, and great in power, and will not at all acquit the wicked.

But thou, Lord, art a God full of compassion, and gracious, long-suffering, and plenteous in mercy and truth.

O, how great is thy goodness which thou hast laid up for them that fear thee !

The righteous cry, and the Lord heareth, and delivereth them out of all their troubles.

When I said, My foot slippeth, thy mercy, O Lord, held me up.

I will praise thee, O Lord my God, with all my heart; and I will glorify thy name forevermore.

I will sing of the mercies of the Lord forever.

O, satisfy us early with thy mercy; that we may rejoice and be glad all our days.

O, come let us worship and bow down: let us kneel before the Lord our Maker.

Morning.

FATHER of mercies, we thank thee yet again for thy kindness. That we are all here together to unite in prayer and in thankfulness, we praise thee. That thou hast given us a happy home, and hast bound us together in the ties of thine own dear love, we thank thee. Forgive us that we ever try to break those ties in our impatience or anger. Forgive us for our passionate words, or for our unkind acts. And grant that to-day we may all live together as thine own children should, giving each to each of the blessings thou hast given to us, and thankful each to each for all that we receive from each other. So be pleased, each day, to make this home thine own home, to lead us all with a Father's hand, and in our faith, and hope, and love here to bring us nearer and nearer to thyself. We ask it and hope for it, trusting in the promises of thy Son. *Amen.*

EVENING.

GOD of all comfort and strength, we know that thou drawest near to thy children who seek thee, in their hours of trial and solicitude. When fond earthly hopes fail, thou, in thine unchangeable goodness and thy all-perfect compassion, dost lift upon us the light of thy countenance, to give us peace. Of thy goodness it is that our life is continued. From thee is the source of every cheering hope of the future. And thou, in thy far-reaching providence, art touching our hearts in all the ways by which we are called to set our affections less upon things of the earth, and things which perish with the using, and to set them more upon what is unfailing and eternal in the heavens. By all the discipline of life thou wouldst bring us closer to thee. We would feel that in the best earthly friendships, and in the nearest ties of human kindred, we see but an imperfect token of the infinite tenderness of thy compassion. Grant that we may with all confidence commit to thee what belongs to the welfare of our household and of the friends whom we love. Grant that we may rest with quietness of heart upon all the disposals made by the Wisdom which is so much higher than ours. May we be happy in the certainty that thou wilt, hereafter, show us what now we know not. Prepare us to be partakers of that higher life which is to be revealed. Of thy tender mercy, forgive whatever is unworthy in us. Bring us into the fulness of thy light and peace, and let there be upon our lips and in our hearts a new song, even praise unto our God. *Amen.*

LVIII.

FAITH IN CHRIST.

My hope is built on nothing less
Than Jesus' blood and righteousness;
I dare not trust the sweetest frame,
But wholly lean on Jesus' name.
On Christ, the solid Rock, I stand;
All other ground is sinking sand.

                                        REES.

Whosoever believeth in Jesus Christ shall not perish, but have eternal life.

Who is he that overcometh the world, but he that believeth that Jesus is the Son of God.

I believe: Lord, increase my faith; and let it be unto thy servant according to this word. — *Wilson.*

For there is one God, and one Mediator between God and man, the man Christ Jesus.

Wherefore God hath highly exalted him, and given him a name which is above every name; that at the name of Jesus every knee should bow, and every tongue should confess that Jesus Christ is Lord, to the glory of God the Father.

I will follow thee whithersoever thou goest:

If thou passest through the fire, I will not be torn from thee :

I will fear no evil since thou art with me. — *St. Bernard.*

A man is not justified by the works of the law, but by the faith of Jesus Christ: even we have believed in Jesus Christ, that we might be justified by the faith of Christ.

But if while we seek to be justified by Christ, we ourselves also are found sinners, is therefore Christ the minister of sin ? God forbid.

Ye are all the children of God by faith in Christ Jesus.

I count all things but loss for the excellency of the knowledge of Christ Jesus my Lord.

That I may win Christ, and be found in him, not having mine own righteousness, which is of the law, but that which is through the faith of Christ, the righteousness which is of God through faith.

MORNING.

O GOD, the God and Father of our Lord Jesus Christ, in the morning, now we have awoke from our death-like slumber, shalt thou again hear our voice. The light of a new day, sent forth by thee, and spread over earth and sea and sky, is again shining into our dwellings : let the light of thy truth shine in our hearts, and may there be in us no darkness at all. The air savors of thy love, bird and beast sing of thy wisdom, and incense is going up to thee from ten thousand urns ; how ungrateful we must be, how cold and dead, if we can now be dumb and have no offerings of praise to thee, who hast formed us with susceptibility of enjoyment, imparted to the bosom its tenderness, and given a voice of harmony to all thy creation. Open thou our lips. Teach us to pray. And may our prayers, prompted and framed by thee, go up on the wings of devotion, and on the sweet breath of the morning.

Our Father who art in heaven, blessed be thy name for what the day brings, for the renewed manifestations of thy wisdom and the fresh tokens of thy watchful providence and unchanging love. Seated in thy high and holy place, thou dost guide the great orbs of light along their wondrous paths, bringing to us the morning and the evening and the vicissitudes of the seasons. Thou dost order the events of every life ; and not a flower blossoms nor a sparrow falls without the notice of thine eye. Above all, do we thank thee for that sweet influence which informs, guides, and sustains. The law came by Moses, but truth and grace by Jesus Christ. Not only hast thou given us the fair world, full of riches and varied enjoyments, to live in ; but a world, sanctified by the presence, cheered by the sacred words and works, and hallowed by the footsteps, the tears, and the blood of thy Son. Blessed be thy name beyond all present enjoyment, — all that may please the eye and the ear and the grosser

senses : what hast thou not done to soothe the solici-
tudes and satisfy the deeper wants of the heart !
Thou hast bowed the very heavens and come down ;
and what tender associations, what precious memories, what transcendent hopes, hast thou imparted
to kindle within us the religious life, to lift us above
these transient scenes, and bear us away to those
immortal regions where thou wilt unveil thy glory,
and satisfy the craving heart of man.

O Lord, most merciful and gracious, do thou this
day strengthen our faith in Jesus ; enlarge our conceptions of the dignity of his office, the sanctity of
his work, the beauty of his life. Let his name be
more and more dear to our hearts. Let the spirit
of his life more and more mould our own. May
we be transformed into his likeness, and feel the
greatness of his love, and so darkness and fear and
despondency be scattered. Infinite Father, may
thy kingdom, which is the kingdom of light and
praise and love, come, thy will be done as it is done
in heaven ; and thine shall be the praise and the
glory forever. *Amen.*

EVENING.

OUR Heavenly Father ! we unite as a household
in thanksgivings to thee for all the blessings
of another day. And while we supplicate thy
merciful care and protection through the hours of

night, we would humbly acknowledge our own weakness and sinfulness, and pray for thy pardoning grace. Thou art a just God and a Saviour. We rejoice that thou hast revealed thyself to us in Jesus Christ, as mighty to save and ready to forgive. Help us through him to find our way to thee, as the loving Father of our spirits. May thy Holy Spirit interpret to us more clearly the gospel of salvation. May our souls be washed and purified in the healing fountains of thy love. May the peace of God be richly shed abroad in our hearts as we go to our nightly rest. Bless us with the sweet assurance that we are the companions of angels, that thine own everlasting arm is about us, and that thine unslumbering eye watches over us for good. Refresh us in body and soul. Prepare us, through thine inworking grace, for all future duties and trials. And when all earthly things shall fail with us, O admit us to be joint heirs with Jesus Christ to thine everlasting kingdom. *Amen.*

LIX.

SEARCH THE SCRIPTURES.

It is the one true Light
That, when all other lamps grow dim,
Shall never burn less purely bright,
Nor lead astray from. Him.

It is the golden Key
To treasures of celestial wealth, —
Joy to the sons of poverty,
And to the sick man, health.

EMILY TAYLOR.

Search the Scriptures; for in them ye think ye have eternal life: and they are they which testify of me.

If thou desire to reap profit, read with humility, simplicity, and faithfulness; nor ever desire the estimation of learning. — *À Kempis.*

For whatsoever things were written aforetime, were written for our learning, that we, through patience and comfort of the Scriptures, might have hope.

Continue in the things which thou hast learned, and hast been assured of.

The Holy Scriptures are able to make thee wise unto salvation, through faith which is in Christ Jesus.

The Holy Scriptures have not only an elementary use, but a use of perfection; neither can they ever be exhausted, but still, even to the most learned and perfect in them, there is somewhat to be learned more. — *Herbert.*

From hardness of heart, and contempt of thy Word, good Lord deliver us. — *Wilson.*

He that saith I know God, and keepeth not his commandments, is a liar, and the truth is not in him.

But whoso keepeth his word, in him verily is the love of God perfected.

Give me, O God, a sincere love for the truths of the Gospel, a teachable heart, and an obedient will.

Order my steps in thy word : and let not any iniquity have dominion over me.

Let my heart be sound in thy statutes; that I be not ashamed.

The word of the Lord endureth forever; and this is the word which by the gospel is preached unto you.

Morning.

O THOU incomprehensible Being, whose greatness transcends human thought, and whose wisdom is unfathomable, we know thee not as thou art, and may not presume to speak of thy mysterious essence : for who by searching can find out God? But blessed be thy name, thou hast not left thyself without witnesses of thy majesty and memorials of thy goodness. Day unto day uttereth speech, and night unto night showeth knowledge of thee. Thy word hath gone out unto the ends of the earth, and there is no spot so high, so low, or so distant, on which it may not be heard. Thou hast written it on the face of nature, in the courses of the heavenly bodies, on the rocky foundations of our globe, in the changes of the world and the history of man; and they tell of the length of thy years, of the majesty of thy power, and of the greatness of thy wisdom and love.

But, above all, hast thou been pleased to breathe it into the ear of patriarch, prophet, and apostle, and hast caused that it should be inscribed by their hands, and transmitted from generation to generation for our use. How shall we sufficiently thank thee, Holy Father, that these Scriptures, so full of inspiration, and so intimately connected with the life of the world, should be preserved for us. Teach us to value them as we ought. Let us never forget that they contain thy word of truth and thy gracious promise made to the heart of man. Let us remember what they have been to our world; how, when it was lying in ignorance, and under the shadow of death, they guided and instructed and saved it. Let us never forget, that they contain the history of thy communications with man, informed, inspired, and pervaded by thine own spirit, — the promises unto the fathers by the prophets, and their fulfilment in the wonderful life and transcendent works of Jesus, in the unspeakably grand and affecting circumstances which attended his death, resurrection, and ascension to thee, where he ever liveth, at the head of his spiritual kingdom, to guide its destinies, and make intercession for us, and welcome us to his rest.

Merciful Father, save us from the folly of turning away in indifference and neglect from these venerable Scriptures. May we never forget that they contain the word, and are the power of God unto salvation. May we hold them in our heart's reverence. May they be a lamp to our feet, and a guide to our ways. May we search them diligently, and partake largely of their spirit. Open, O God, the inward eye, and we shall see wonderful things out of thy holy word. Open the inward ear, and in all times of our tribulation and self-abandonment, we shall hear thy gentle voice of solace, forgiveness, and peace. Speak, Lord, to our hearts, and it shall be well with thy servants. All of which we ask in the name and as disciples of Jesus Christ. *Amen.*

EVENING.

OUR Father, and our God: thou who dwellest in light ineffable and full of glory; at the close of another day we, thy children, come unto thee to acknowledge our dependence and to seek thy blessing. In our darkness and our ignorance we are prone to go astray; and as this day we have sinned against thee, wilt thou forgive us, and wilt thou send down thy Holy Spirit into our hearts to turn us away from all transgression, and to enlighten our understandings.

We thank thee, our Heavenly Father, for thy truth. Thy word is truth ; and in it we have everlasting life. Give us, we beseech thee, the disposition to search it diligently, and an understanding heart in reading its lessons. As thou hast given it to us to be a lamp unto our feet, and a light unto our path, help us to follow its shining unto the end. In its revelations concerning thee, our Father, and in its revelations concerning a future world, and in what it teaches concerning life and duty, we have full assurance of thy interest in us, and thy care for us, and of thy unfailing solicitude that we should walk in thy commandments and ordinances blameless. If hitherto we have been indifferent to thy word, and have failed to make it our wisdom and our counsel, wilt thou incline our hearts to it henceforth, that we may do the things which it commands, and may be followers together of our Lord Jesus Christ. O God, we need the teachings of thy Spirit, that we may rightly search and duly understand thy word, and that it may lead us in filial obedience and love unto thee, our Father, and conduct us at last to our heavenly home. Wilt thou grant unto us what we so much need, and crown with blessing all our searchings into thy truth.

Our prayer for our friends, for all whom we should remember at the throne of thy grace, for all mankind, is that they may come to a knowledge of the truth, and be everlastingly saved by thy grace.

11*

Do thou hear us, O God, and accept and bless us. We ask it in the name of our Lord and Saviour Jesus Christ. *Amen.*

LX.

TEMPERANCE AND MODERATION.

Happy the man whose cautious steps
  Still keep the golden mean ;
Whose life, by wisdom's rules well formed,
  Declares a conscience clean.

His business is to keep his heart,
  Each passion to control ;
Nobly ambitious well to rule
  The empire of his soul.
                                NEEDHAM.

Let your moderation be known unto all men.

He is fit to sit at the table of the Lord, and to feast with saints, who moderately uses the creatures which God hath given him;

But he that despises even lawful pleasures shall not only sit and feast with God, but reign together with him, and partake of his glorious kingdom. — *Taylor.*

Moderation is the silken string running through the pearl chain of all virtues. — *Fuller.*

Let our life be moderate, our desires reasonable, our hopes little. — *Taylor.*

Be not self-willed, not soon angry, not given to wine, no striker, not given to filthy lucre;

But a lover of hospitality, a lover of good men, sober, just, holy, temperate.

The servant of the Lord must not strive; but be gentle unto all men, apt to teach, patient.

The fruit of the Spirit is love, joy, peace, long-suffering, gentleness, goodness, faith, meekness, temperance.

Be not among wine-bibbers, among riotous eaters of flesh: for the drunkard and the glutton shall come to poverty.

Let us watch and be sober.

He that resisteth pleasure crowneth his life.

Let us not imagine that excess, luxury, and superfluity, and the love of pleasures, are less criminal because so common. — *Wilson.*

Having food and raiment, let us be therewith content.

Morning.

WITH the return of this morning light, O God, we rise, refreshed with slumber, the gift of thy love, to the duties of the day. We direct our prayer unto thee, asking for wisdom and strength to do our duty in all things. O restrain us from all excesses. Make us earnest and firm indeed, but also keep us within the limits of moderation and prudence. Let not our indolence or unbelief cause us to fall short of the mark of our obligation. Let not our rash desires hurry us beyond the sacred boundaries of justice, purity, and our true interests. We pray that through this day, and through every day thy grace allots us below, we may be temperate and judicious in all things, careful to do what shall be pleasing in thy sight. Accept our homage and answer our petitions, O Lord, for thy mercy's sake in Jesus Christ our Lord. *Amen.*

EVENING.

ALMIGHTY God, Father of our spirits, we thank thee for all the powers and faculties of our nature; for those capacities by which we are distinguished from the brutes that perish. Grant us, we pray thee, an entire control over all our dispositions and desires, that we may never come into bondage to our appetites, nor be swayed by the objects of flesh and sense. By thy gracious aid may we be enabled to maintain a conscience void of offence towards God and towards man. Aid us to be perpetually vigilant in the examination of our motives and the government of our actions. May we bridle the tongue in every hour of temptation, remembering that, if any man offend not in word, the same is a perfect man. Give us an eye to see ourselves as we are seen by others, and, above all, by thee the Omniscient One.

Holy Father, we pray for a complete knowledge of our ruling principles and affections; may we discern clearly our chief moral dangers, and become acquainted with our transgressions and our defects. Clothe us with more power over the great springs of our conduct; give us, we beseech thee, daily new victories over our corrupt passions and irregular desires. Let us rise continually toward that elevated condition where no prejudices will distort our judgment, no unkind emotions enter our breasts, and nothing impure exist within us to disturb our peace.

We thank thee that, in this our earthly warfare with evil, we have as a forerunner One who was tempted as we are at all points, yet escaped without sin. We pray for the same mind which was also in our Lord and Saviour Jesus Christ. Let his constant self-denial dwell in us, that we may subject ourselves, like him, wholly to thy will. In all the changing scenes of life may his blessed Gospel, by its sacred truths, its perfect precepts, and its glorious promises, be a light to our feet, and enable us to resist temptation, and bear us up under every trial, sorrow, and burden. In the evil day may we be led on by thine invisible hand, and delivered in safety from our spiritual foes. Help us to use this world as not abusing it, seeing that the fashion of it passeth quickly away. Chasten all our expectations and hopes; and may we let our moderation be known unto all men. Free from our unholy ambition, and loving thy praise more than the praise of man, may we never be unduly elevated by human praise or depressed by the ill opinion of others. Caring more to deserve approbation than to receive it, we desire to seek supremely that honor which cometh from on high. In the conflicts and struggles before us, aid us, we beseech thee, by thy Holy Spirit, that we may come off more than conquerors through Him who hath loved us, in whose name we ascribe unto thee glory and praise forever. *Amen.*

LXI.

LEAD US NOT INTO TEMPTATION.

Veil, Lord, mine eyes till she be past,
When Folly tempts my sight;
Keep thou my palate and my taste
From gluttonous delight;
Stop thou mine ear from sirens' songs,
My tongue from lies restrain;
Withhold my hands from doing wrongs,
My feet from courses vain.
GEORGE WITHER.

Every man is tempted when he is drawn away of his own lust, and enticed.

Blessed is the man that endureth temptation; for when he is tried, he shall receive the crown of life, which the Lord hath promised to them that love him.

Watch and pray, that ye enter not into temptation.

We must not be surprised that we are tempted. We are placed here to be proved by temptations. Everything is temptation to us. Crosses irritate our pride, and prosperity flatters it; our life is a continual warfare; but Jesus Christ combats with us. — *Fénelon.*

Temptations are often very profitable to us, though they be troublesome and grievous; for in them a man is humbled, purified, and instructed. — *À Kempis.*

The beginning of all evil temptations is inconstancy of mind and small confidence in God. — *À Kempis.*

If you would not be foiled by temptation, do not enter into a dispute with Satan. Dispute not, but fight. — *Anon.*

God is faithful, who will not suffer you to be tempted above that ye are able, but will with the temptation also make a way to escape, that ye may be able to bear it.

Let us not, then, shrink from these trials, remembering always that in them Jesus Christ fights with us, and for us. — *St. Chrysostom.*

Him that overcometh will I make a pillar in the temple of my God, and he shall go no more out; and I will write upon him the name of my God, and the name of the city of my God, which is new Jerusalem.

Set a watch, O Lord, before my mouth; keep the door of my lips.

Incline not my heart to any evil thing, to practise wicked works with men that work iniquity.

MORNING.

O HOLY Father, by whose loving-kindness we have been thus far led, and by whose good providence we see the returning light of this day, let thy light shine ever upon our path, — that marvellous light which is from above, and which shall show us all things in their true character. Let thy dear Son this day touch the eyes of each one of us, that they may be opened to detect every illusion of the tempter, and preserve us from all his snares. We have neither strength nor wisdom in ourselves, O Father, but in thy grace through Christ Jesus we can do all things. Fulfil for us his prayer, that his disciples may be with him where he is. And in the light of his word and of his presence let us behold the reality of things of the Spirit, the emptiness and falsehood of the promises of the flesh ; by the strength of thy grace may we be strong this day to walk in the path of duty, to hold fast our integrity, and to resist every allurement to evil, however closely it may assume the garb of an angel of light.

O Father, show thy mercy unto all thy children, bringing forth among all nations truth victorious, and causing justice to prevail against wrong-doers ; hastening in every land the coming of thy kingdom. Let our own land, O gracious God, be ever dealt with in mercy, and all our nation brought into the ways of righteousness and liberty and peace. And may thy blessing be upon us and upon all whom we love, this day and evermore. *Amen.*

HEAVENLY Father, we implore thy blessing, surrounded as we are by a world of temptation and danger. Give us, we beseech thee, that wisdom which is from above, that we may be able to discern between the things that differ in thy sight, and to choose always that which is right. May we take fast hold of instruction, and not let her go ; may we keep her, knowing that she is our life. May we incline our ear to wisdom, and apply our heart to understanding, and depart from all evil. Preserve us from that pride which goeth before destruction, and from that haughty spirit which precedeth a fall. Guard us from undue confidence in our own wisdom when apart from thee ; endow us with a meek and teachable disposition, that we may look up to thee for help in every hour of exposure and peril. Ever may we watch against the approach of our spiritual enemies, putting on the whole armor of faith and salvation. We would listen reverently to the admonition and reproof of conscience, and to the voice of thy Son, our dear Saviour. By acknowledging and forsaking our past errors, may we be saved and shielded against future sins. Thou art teaching us daily by the course of thy providence and the secret counsels of thy Holy Spirit ; let not these solemn lessons be ever lost upon us.

Give us an eye to see the constant evidence there is of thy moral government over us, and that thou, the Righteous One, lovest righteousness and hatest iniquity. May we be thoroughly convinced that there is no true and lasting peace to those who do evil, and that it is always well with those who keep thy commandments. Thou art our Father, help us to be thy loving and obedient children, rejoicing to know thy blessed will, and to do it with our whole hearts. We would submit ourselves to the guidance of thy unerring counsels, and pray that none of the deceitful pleasures of sin may seduce us into the path of the transgressor. Establish thou us in the firm control of our passions, and the steady government of our hearts and our whole lives. Help us to discern the certainty and the value of the recompense thou hast prepared for persevering virtue, and to know by our own happy experience that in keeping thy commands there is a present and great reward. Let our views of thee be so clear and so tender and affecting that we shall never grow weary of well-doing. Now unto Him who is able to keep us from falling, and to present us without blame before the presence of his glory with exceeding joy, to God only wise, be glory forever. *Amen.*

LXII.

PRAY WITHOUT CEASING.

. Prayer is the soul's sincere desire,
Uttered or unexpressed ;
The motion of a hidden fire
That trembles in the breast.
MONTGOMERY.

Verily I say unto you, Whatsoever ye shall ask the Father in my name, he will give it you.

Ask, and it shall be given you; seek, and ye shall find; knock, and it shall be opened unto you.

This is the confidence we have in God, that if we ask anything according to his will, he heareth us.

How good is God! who will not only give us what we pray for, but will reward us for going to him, and laying our wants before him. — *Wilson.*

May I wait with patience, and leave it to thee *how* and *when* to grant my petitions. — *Wilson.*

To pray is to say, Let thy will be done; it is to form a good purpose; it is to raise our hearts to God; it is to lament our weakness; it is to sigh at the recollection of our frequent disobedience. — *Fénelon.*

Ask not for that which is delightful and profitable to thee, but for that which is acceptable to God;

For those desires are not pure and perfect which are tinctured with the love of thine own special interest and advantage. — *À Kempis.*

Prayers are but the body of the bird; desires are its angel's wings. — *Taylor.*

What is the Almighty, saith the wicked, that we should serve him? and what profit should we have if we pray unto him?

From the few hours we spend in prayer and the exercises of a pious life the return is great and profitable; and what we sow in the minutes and spare portions of a few years, grows up to crowns and sceptres in a happy and glorious eternity. — *Taylor.*

The heart without the tongue may pierce the ears of heaven, the tongue without the heart speaks an unknown language. Rather speak three words in a speech that God knows, than pray three hours in a language that he understands not. — *Warwick.*

Pray without ceasing; not in mere words, but in so living united to God, in your affections and thoughts, that your life shall be one long and continued prayer. — *St. Basil.*

MORNING.

O THOU who art our life and the length of our days, may we at all times set thee before us in everything we design, do, or undertake. In every period of our life we would avail ourselves of those opportunities which are suited to enlarge our conceptions of thee, and to acquaint us with our whole duty to thee, to show us our dependence, to correct our wrong inclinations, to guard us against false and criminal suggestions, and to confirm us in all good principles and habits. In whatever employments we may engage, or into whatever relations we may enter, O keep thou us constantly aware of thy presence, and mindful that this is but a preparatory scene, and that our preparation for another life will consist in the proper discharge of the duties of the present.

Thou, O God, art full of truth, purity, holiness, and love! Pour down these great gifts continually, we pray thee, upon us. Shed upon us every hour of our lives thy renewing and sanctifying power, that our minds may be lifted toward thee while our hands are occupied with life's tasks. Let our hearts be so filled with the love of thy law, that we shall hate all vain thoughts, and shun whatever would lead us to wander from thy commandments. Be thou our hiding-place in danger, and our shield against the subtlety and evil influence of others, that they may never, by their persuasions or example, ensnare our souls. We implore thee to be our strength and our stay, that we may always walk with the wise and the pure, and find our delight in being with them that love thee.

God and Father of our Lord Jesus Christ, help us to be one with him as he is one with thee, that we may enjoy, like him, the sweet consciousness that thou hearest us always. We ask for an ever firm faith in all the truths thou didst send him to teach. May we daily hear thy voice remind us through him

of the glorious life which is to come. In our lonely
hours, may we learn of him to feel that we are not
alone, for the Father is with us. Amid our cares
and engagements, may we realize that we shall be
in nothing profited, if we gain the world and lose
our own souls. In our amusements and pleasures
we would hear him bidding us look to thee lest our
hearts be drawn off from duty and heaven. When
trouble and sorrow come upon us, may we not be
cast down, but turn to thee, and find the consolation
we need. So may we live, that all our thoughts
shall be ordered as before thee, and thou be the joy
of our joys and the peace of our griefs. May we
rest calmly in thine hands under all the checkered
scenes of this world, and gaze steadfastly toward that
kingdom without beginning and without end. Hear
us, we beseech thee, through Christ our Redeemer.
Amen.

EVENING.

OUR Heavenly Father! thou blessed Spirit in
whom we live and move and have our being!
we come to thee at the close of another day and
seek thy blessing. The night is falling on the weary
world, and a holy calm, a religious repose, seems to
fill the twilight, and whisper to our souls of thy nearness and love. O Father, at this quiet, thoughtful
hour, may our hearts be filled with that peace which
the world cannot give nor take away. May we be

grateful for the blessings of this day, for health and
home and friends; or even for the discipline of sorrow, pain, and disappointment; for all things through
which we are called back from our wanderings and
drawn nearer to our better selves and to thee. We
are penitent of our sins; we feel oppressed and dis-
couraged to think how we forget thee day after day;
we do aspire and pray for a better and more success-
ful life than that which we now live. O we bless
thee that thou art so patient with us! That thy
spirit is not grieved away by all our failures and sins.
Infinite pity, patience, love, darkness, and sadness
gather on our souls as we think of our unworthiness,
and we fly for shelter under the shadow of thy wing.
May faith and hope shine upon our darkness as the
stars are shining on this night! In our weakness may
we find strength, in our darkness may we find light;
in our ignorance may we find knowledge in thee.
Guard our slumbers when we lie down to sleep.
May thoughts of heaven visit us even in our dreams,
that we may meditate upon thee in the night-watches. Be with all who are dear to us this night. Save
them from dangers seen and unseen; may we feel
ourselves united in thee, however widely we are separated in all earthly relations. Forgive our sins,
and purify our souls, that we may see thee and love
thee and feel thy helpful presence ever near in our
weakness; and to thy name shall be all the glory
and honor for ever and ever. *Amen.*

LXIII.

FEAR GOD.

Great God! how infinite art thou!
How frail and weak are we!
Let the whole race of creatures bow,
And homage pay to thee.

WATTS.

Blessed is the man that feareth the Lord; that delighteth greatly in his commandments.

In the faithful soul the fear of the Lord consists entirely in love; and the principal duty of that love is to obey his commandments and believe his promises. — *St. Hilary.*

The Lord taketh pleasure in them that fear him, in those that hope in his mercy.

The fear of the Lord is to hate evil.

The fear of the Lord prolongeth days; but the years of the wicked shall be cut off.

In the fear of the Lord is strong confidence; and his children shall have a place of refuge.

They that feared the Lord spake often one to another; and the Lord hearkened, and heard it, and a book of remembrance was written before him for them that feared the Lord, and that thought upon his name.

And they shall be mine, saith the Lord of hosts, in that day when I make up my jewels.

What man is he that feareth the Lord? him shall he teach in the way that he shall choose.

His soul shall dwell at ease ; and his seed shall inherit the earth.

The secret of the Lord is with them that fear him ; and he will show them his covenant.

Who fears God will find himself elevated above the terrors and menaces of this world, — they are for him only vain phantoms, which he despises, and speedily disperses. — *St. Ephraim.*

Blessed is the man that feareth the Lord, that delighteth greatly in his commandments.

Let us hear the conclusion of the whole matter : Fear God, and keep his commandments ; for this is the whole duty of man.

For the mercy of the Lord is from everlasting to everlasting upon them that fear him, and his righteousness unto children's children.

MORNING.

WE adore thee, O Lord, for we are fearfully and wonderfully made, fearfully and wonderfully preserved. Thou compassest our path and our lying down and art acquainted with all our ways. As the sun this morning again darts his searching ray from one end of the heavens to the other, and makes visible the things which had been hidden in darkness, so does the eye of thy holy Son search our consciences and all the windings of our hearts. For there is not a thought or a desire there, but lo, O Lord, thou knowest it altogether. If thou, Lord, shouldst mark iniquities, who should stand? But there is forgiveness with thee, that thou mayest be feared. May thy goodness, thy holiness, thy greatness, conspire to make us afraid to sin against thy pure spirit, against the nature in which thou hast made us, against the sacred relations in which thou hast bound us to thy family on earth. May we be afraid of the sin of hiding in the earth the talent thou hast intrusted to us; may we dread the shadow of a stain upon our souls. Cleanse us, O God, from every secret fault. May our filial fear of thee swallow up all other fear. May we be piously afraid to let the fear of the world deter us from the straight path of childlike and Christian simplicity, may we this day do justly, love mercy and walk humbly with thee, our God. Create in us, O God, a clean heart, renew a right spirit within us; if there be any wicked way in us, forgive and correct it, and lead us in the way everlasting, through Christ. *Amen.*

EVENING.

O GOD, thou infinite one, who dwellest among the sanctities of heaven and in the midst of thy matchless perfections, whom no eye hath seen, whose greatness no human mind can compass, and whose love no human heart can fathom, all honor and reverence and answering affection be rendered unto thee. In the silence and solemnity of the evening hour we come once more, the members of this Christian family, to the place of our refuge, our endeared family altar.

And Holy Father, how can we come before thee but to put our hands on our mouths and our mouths in the dust? Another day is gone, with its precious hours of light in which to walk, with its vast opportunities of usefulness and means of improvement, with trusts that cannot be measured and burdens of responsibility and demands of duty that cannot be weighed; and when in the quiet of our meditations we take council with ourselves, and reflect upon the magnitude of thy gifts and the poorness of our services, how can we stand before thee but with added shame and humiliation? Thou hast prolonged the lives which our consciences tell us have been all too meanly devoted, and spared the blessings which we have but too freely abused. Thou hast said to us, " My son, give me thy heart," and, lo, we have too seldom had thee in all our thoughts. Thou hast said to us, " Go work in my vineyard," and behold, we have been idle and slothful, while the fields have been white for the harvest. We feel that we have not been eyes to the blind, garments to the naked, and feet to the weary, as we should have been. In the multitude of our wayward thoughts and earth-born cares, we have failed and fallen short in our duty to thee. We come, therefore, not to justify ourselves, but to ask pardon of thee. Lift, O God,

the burden of our conscious deficiency. Have
mercy upon us, and blot our sins from the book of
thy remembrance.

For what are we that we should a single moment
be forgetful of thee, and transgress thy most righteous laws? Our constant Preserver and most bountiful Benefactor, thou mayest justly claim our entire
service. Former of our bodies, Father of our
spirits, and Disposer of our lot, help us ever to stand
in awe, and sin not; and as we shall meditate upon
thee on our beds, let us feel more of thy pervading presence and thine incomprehensible greatness.
From our own mean estate we turn our eyes upwards; we gaze into the mysterious depth, — on the
boundless expanse of these heavens, the moon walking in her brightness, and the stars holding their silent watch, — on thyself more wondrous still, guiding worlds on worlds through eternity; and we are
utterly overwhelmed by the grandeur of our con-
templations. What is man, that thou art mindful
of him, or the Son of man, that thou shouldest visit
him!

We lay our hearts lowly before thee. We ask
for thy tender pity, and the watch of thine unslumbering eye, and the shelter of thy protecting wing.
Amen.

LXIV.

THY WAYS ARE NOT OUR WAYS.

Thy ways, O Lord, with wise design,
Are framed upon thy throne above,
And every dark or bending line
Meets in the centre of thy love.
ANONYMOUS.

Beware thou dispute not of high matters, nor of the secret judgments of God, why this man is so left, and that man taken into such great favor; why also one is so grievously afflicted, and another so eminently exalted. — *À Kempis.*

These things are beyond all reach of man's faculties, neither is it in the power of any reason or disputation to search out the judgments of God. — *À Kempis.*

For my thoughts are not your thoughts, neither are your ways my ways, saith the Lord.

For as the heaven is higher than the earth, so are my ways higher than your ways, and my thoughts higher than your thoughts. The wisdom of men is foolishness with God.

The ways of the Lord are right, and the just shall walk in them; but the transgressors shall fall therein.

Canst thou by searching find out God? canst thou find out the Almighty to perfection?

Hast thou not known, hast thou not heard, that the everlasting God, the Lord, the creator of the ends of the earth, fainteth not, neither is weary? There is no searching of his understanding.

Where is the wise? where is the scribe? where is the disputer of this world? hath not God made foolish the wisdom of this world?

Faith is required at thy hands, and a sincere life; not height of understanding, nor the depth of the mysteries of God.— *À Kempis.*

Far be it from God, that he should do wickedness; and from the Almighty, that he should commit iniquity.

For the work of a man shall he render unto him, and cause every man to find according to his ways.

O the depth of the riches both of the wisdom and the knowledge of God! How unsearchable are his judgments, and his ways past finding out.

For of him, and through him, and to him are all things; to whom be glory forever.

MORNING.

ALMIGHTY God, it is through thy tender care that we have been spared to see this day. Gratefully we would dwell upon the thought of thy constant presence.

We rejoice to feel that thou art about our path, and art acquainted with all our ways. That thou, who didst create us, art ever watching over us; and that thou, who knowest the avenues to our hearts, art always gently approaching and breathing over us the influences of thy spirit. Confirm our faith in thee and thy providences.

Be with us, we beseech thee, now, when, refreshed by the interval of rest from our daily cares, we go forth to them anew.

Thou knowest, O God, the temptations we are to meet. Thou knowest how hard it is to keep always mindful of what is right; how our thoughts fasten on earthly things, while the clouds of passion shut out from us the light of heavenly truth; how the passing allurements of the world smother the higher yearnings of the soul.

We would not go out without the guidance and support of thy helping spirit. We pray thee that we may receive that strength which is not our own, which alone can make us strong against the evil to which we shall be exposed.

Bless us in all our worthy pursuits. Hallow all our enjoyments. Sanctify all the experiences we may be called to meet. We joyfully submit ourselves to thy guidance, certain of thy love and care for us. Lead us in thy truth, and teach us, O thou God of our salvation. Guide us by thy counsel, and finally receive us into glory. We ask it, for Christ's sake. *Amen.*

EVENING.

O THOU all-wise and all-merciful One, the ways are past finding out; thy purposes of grace are infinitely beyond our finite thought. We would banish every fear and doubt, while we adore thy sovereign wisdom. At the close of every day we would resign ourselves to thy fatherly hand. Amidst all the mysteries of life, we would rest upon thy infinite love. How graciously hast thou always guided our wayward steps. As we look back over our lives, light breaks out of darkness, and we see that thou wert teaching us while we knew it not, and blessing us through our disappointments and our griefs, and looking upon us under the shadows of every cloud, with thine eye of love.

Infinite Father, we know not whether to give thee greater thanks for adversity or prosperity, for grief or joy, since every dispensation is another revelation of the same incomprehensible mercy. But we do bless thee that thou overrulest our steps, and dost not leave us to our shortsightedness and folly. We bless thee for thy rebukes to our passion and our pride, for all the chastisements of thy loving hand. We would adore and give thanks where we cannot see, and ask not for what we may foolishly wish, but for strength according to our day.

Holy Father, inspired by such thoughts as these, may we find grace always to yield ourselves to thy sovereign guidance with a cheerful and childlike trust. May we be ready to follow wherever thou shalt lead, and to take up every cross which thou shalt ordain. Teach us, in the spirit of thy dear Son, to say, not our will, but thine be done. Help us to wait patiently for the unfoldings of thy will, for the perfect revelation of the mysteries of thy perfect love. May we feel it to be enough for us now to know that we can never be alone in the darkest hour, because thou art always with us still. And so may we find thy acceptance now, and thy acceptance forever in that world in which faith will give place to sight, through Jesus Christ our Lord. *Amen.*

LXV.

SELF–DENIAL.

> *Our flesh and sense must be denied,*
> *Passion and envy, lust and pride,*
> *While justice, temperance, truth, and love*
> *Our inward piety approve.*
> WATTS.

Go not after thy lusts, but refrain thyself from thine appetites. Delight thyself in the Lord, and he shall give thee the desires of thine heart.

Jesus said, If a man will come after me, let him deny himself, and take up his cross and follow me.

He that loveth pleasure shall be a poor man.

He that resisteth pleasure, crowneth his life.

He that keepeth himself subject, in such sort that his sensual affections be obedient to reason, and his reason in all things obedient to God, that person is truly conqueror of himself, and lord of the world. — *À Kempis.*

When thou degradest thyself by low affections, thou puttest thyself on a level, in thy inclinations, with irrational beasts; thy soul assumes their likeness. Thou art called to nobler destinies; seek, then, the Most High, seek Jesus Christ, elevate thy thoughts to heaven. — *St. Basil.*

I know that in me (that is, in my flesh) dwelleth no good thing; for to will is present with me; but how to perform that which is good I find not.

For the good that I would, I do not; but the evil which I would not, that I do.

Wouldest thou that thy flesh obey thy spirit? then let thy spirit obey thy God. Thou must be governed, that thou mayest govern. — *St. Augustine.*

Crucify the man of sin boldly, resolutely, instantly; but crucify him with the cross of Christ, in which is life and salvation. — *St. Bernard.*

For the grace of God that bringeth salvation hath appeared to all men.

Teaching us that, denying ungodliness and worldly lusts, we should live soberly, righteously, and godly in this present world;

Looking for that blessed hope, and the glorious appearing of the great God and our Saviour Jesus Christ.

Morning.

FATHER of light and love! We adore thy majesty, we acknowledge thy perfections, we rejoice in thy goodness. We thank thee for our existence, and that we find our lives continued and renewed unto us at the opening of this new day. May we cheerfully take upon us the yoke of duty, and may we trust in thee for strength to meet all our responsibilities. Teach us the right use of our powers ; may we not profanely squander our strength upon unworthy objects. Help us to resist temptation, and to overcome the lust of the flesh, the lust of the eye, and the pride of life. Deliver us from all low and gross desires, which prevent our hungering and thirsting after spiritual and heavenly things. Anoint our eyes, that we may see the sacredness of all things around us and within us, and sanctify our hearts, that we may enjoy thee in the midst of thy common blessings. Make us strong in the Lord, that we may be masters of ourselves and rule well our own spirits. Through all the excitements and allurements, the cares and activities of the day, may thy peace be in our hearts. May we do justly, love mercy, walk humbly with thee, and keep ourselves unspotted from the world.

Father, thy will be done on earth as it is in heaven. May the right everywhere triumph over the wrong. May our own dear country become a land of righteousness and freedom and peace. May the light of thy Gospel shine in all the nations, and may the kingdoms of this world become the kingdom of our Lord and his Christ. *Amen.*

Evening.

MOST merciful God! Again, at the close of the day, we gather about the family altar, to unite in our evening devotions. We thank thee, our Father, for thy protection over us during the day, for the blessings which have followed us at every step, for the comforts of our lot, for friends and home. But we lament that too often these very gifts of thy bounty have been the means of drawing our thoughts from thee. Immersed in enjoyment of the gifts, we have forgotten the Giver, and so have neglected that active service due to thee, our Maker and Preserver.

And not only have we omitted those things which we ought to have done, but we have done those things which we ought not to have done. We have yielded to temptation, and fallen into sin. For this, O God, pity and forgive us; and do thou, we beseech thee, so impress thine image on our hearts, so take possession of our wills, so attach us to thee by the cords of love, that we may henceforth spurn and reject all pleasures of sense which can in any way offend thee, or defile us, or impose even a shadow of separation between our hearts and thee.

May we be strong to resist temptation; able and willing, — yea, rejoicing to take up and bear any cross appointed us in thine infinite wisdom.

Be with us this night, and leave us not on the morrow. Take up thine abode in our hearts, and drive thence every evil thought, in Christ's name we pray. *Amen.*

LXVI.

SIMPLICITY AND GODLY SINCERITY.

> *Lord, that I may learn of thee,*
> *Give me true simplicity;*
> *Wean my soul, and keep it low,*
> *Willing thee alone to know.*
> METHODIST COL.

By two wings a man is lifted up from things earthly, — by Simplicity and Purity. — *À Kempis.*

Let this be thy whole endeavor, this thy prayer, this thy desire: that thou mayest be stript of all selfishness, and with entire simplicity follow Jesus only. — *À Kempis.*

No man can serve two masters.

I fear, lest by any means, as the serpent beguiled Eve through his subtilty, so your minds should be corrupted from the simplicity that is in Christ.

Will it not please God, that we should surrender our souls to him, without fear or reserve? This deliverance of the soul from all useless and selfish and unquiet cares brings to it a peace and freedom that are unspeakable; this is true simplicity. — *Fénelon.*

For our rejoicing is this, the testimony of our conscience, that in simplicity and godly sincerity, not with fleshly wisdom, but by the grace of God, we have had our conversation in the world.

If there be a joy in the world, surely a man of a pure heart possesseth it. — *À Kempis.*

It is a blessed simplicity when a man leaves the difficult ways of questions and disputings, and goes on forward in the plain and firm path of God's commandments. — *À Kempis.*

God walketh with the simple, revealeth himself to the humble, giveth understanding to the little ones, openeth the sense to pure minds. — *À Kempis.*

The meek shall inherit the earth, and shall delight themselves in the abundance of peace.

Christ teaches that only those who become again, as it were, little children, and by the simplicity of that age cut off the inordinate affections of vice, can enter the kingdom of heaven. — *St. Hilary.*

MORNING.

BEING of infinite purity and truth, thou who dwellest in the heaven of heavens, yet deignest also to make thy home in every humble and trusting heart, we come to thee in the dawning of this new day, to ask that thou wilt lift up the light of thy countenance upon our hearts, to guide us into the way of peace. As the day returns to gladden the world, which it wakes to beauty and joy, so, we pray, let thy Sun of Righteousness shine upon our souls, that we may be awakened to a profound consciousness of thy presence with us, and to a fresh consecration of ourselves to thy simple and sincere service. Let the remembrance of thy mercies, which every morning are renewed to us, sink deeply into our grateful hearts, and move us to give up our entire selves to that single-minded obedience of thee and devotion to thy will, in which alone we can find rest unto our souls.

Thou knowest our every need. The words in which we frame our petitions unto thee, and the unspoken prayers which breathe from our hearts, the crying of our natures unto thee for help, the voice of longing and need which we can utter to no human being, thou hearest and knowest all, and thou canst answer our prayers. We implore thee to shed abroad in our hearts the influences of thy holy spirit, to calm every troubled and unquiet thought. Lead us to love thee with · an entire love. Draw us away from a too engrossing devotion to this world, and make us to estimate it at its true value, by showing us the unspeakable glory of those things which thou hast prepared for those who love thee. When the world attracts us strongly, and pleasure excludes thee from our thoughts, and our minds are set on things which perish, then, we pray, by whatever discipline thou wilt, purify us and recall us to thyself, and enlighten our souls, that we may look beyond what concerns only this mortal life, and humbly and devoutly may seek for the help which cometh from thee. And by this inward preparation fit us to set forth in our outward walk among men the Gospel of Christ which we profess. Enable us to live consistent Christian lives, that we may be known to have been with Jesus and to have infused something of his spirit into our own hearts. Give us the grace to be faithful followers of him amid whatever trials and temptations may befall us, that none of such things may move us from a firm and abiding trust in thee; so that finally we may be received to that heaven of purity and truth and love, for which this world is the preparation, revealed to us by thy Son, Jesus Christ our Lord. *Amen.*

EVENING.

OUR Father in heaven, who knowest how frail we are, and how great is the power of earthly allurements to captivate our thoughts and turn us away from our highest good, forgive our sins, and so endow us with thy spirit and thy grace, that in simplicity and godly sincerity we may have our conversation in the world. Help us to give ourselves entirely to thee, that we may seek no other rule of life but thy truth, that we may have no other ambition but to do thy will, and ask no higher pleasure than the joy of loving and serving thee. Let not the fear or the favor of man, or any inferior interest or passion, stand between our souls and thee. Forgive us if we have failed to live thus in accordance with thy will, and impress upon us, in all time to come, a sense of our perpetual obligation to thee. In thee, O God, is our trust. In thee is our life. Let us not be drawn away from thee, nor from the singleness of purpose and steadfastness of faith which become thy children. May He who is the Resurrection and the Life dwell in our hearts, and may we, rooted and grounded in love, be able to know the love of Christ, which passeth knowledge, and be filled with all the fulness of God. Through thy great mercy in Jesus Christ our Lord. *Amen.*

LXVII.

LOVE TO MAN.

God's law demands one living faith,
Not a gaunt crowd of lifeless creeds :
Its warrant is a firm " God saith," —
Its claim, not words, but loving deeds.

C. A. Briggs.

Love one another with a pure heart fervently.

Let love be without dissimulation. Be kindly affectioned to one another with brotherly love, in honor preferring one another.

Love feels no burden, thinks nothing of trouble, attempts what is above its strength, pleads no excuse of impossibility;

for it thinks all things lawful for itself, and all things possible.
— *À Kempis.*

If a man say I love God, and hateth his brother, he is a liar.
For he that loveth not his brother whom he hath seen, how
can he love God whom he hath not seen ?

And this commandment have we from him, That he who
loveth God, love his brother also.

Love is active, sincere, affectionate, pleasant, and amiable;
courageous, patient, faithful, prudent, long-suffering, manly,
and never seeking itself. — *À Kempis.*

Let brotherly love continue.

Ye have heard that it hath been said, Thou shalt love thy
neighbor and hate thy enemy :

But I say unto you, Love your enemies, bless them that
curse you, do good to them that hate you, and pray for them
which despitefully use you and persecute you.

For if ye love them which love you, what reward have ye ?
do not even the publicans so ?

The Lord make you to increase and abound in love one
toward another, and toward all men.

MORNING.

O THOU who dwellest in light inaccessible and
full of glory, mortal eye hath not seen thee.
With all our searching we cannot find thee out unto
perfection. And yet how graciously hast thou revealed thyself to our hearts, so that our hearts can
understand thee. Thou art our Father! Thou
whose power is limitless, whose knowledge is bound-

less, who art possessed of all things in thyself, —
thou, the Infinite One, — hast encouraged us to know
and worship and confide in thee, as a being of ceaseless love and unwearied compassion. Thou num-
berest the very hairs of our heads, and sendest the
blessing of the sunshine and the rain upon all alike.
Thou art no respecter of persons ; all are thy children. Help us to remember this, by a more faithful
acknowledgment of the ties of the human brotherhood. Since he who loveth not his brother, whom
he hath seen, cannot love God, whom he hath not
seen, give us grace to be just, full of gentle chari-
ties, and kindly affectioned towards our fellow-men,
equally with ourselves unforgotten of thee, and the
objects of thy beneficence. May we do unto others
as we would that others should do unto us. May we
forgive trespasses as we would have our trespasses
forgiven. Save us from selfishness and hardness of
heart. As we share the common lot, may we acknowledge the claims of a common humanity. In
our day and generation may we be faithful to whatever concerns the welfare of our race. Teach us
rightly to serve our neighbor, that thus we may
show forth our gratitude for thy paternal care.
Let us not live to ourselves alone ; but let us live
as members of thy human family, honoring everywhere the nature which thou hast made in thine
own image. May we live the disciples of Him who
hath said, "Inasmuch as ye have done it unto the

least of these my brethren, ye have done it unto me." Hear us, O Father, in this supplication for larger inspirations of love, and thine shall be the praise and the glory forever. *Amen.*

EVENING.

FATHER of infinite love and mercy, again we come to lay before thee a day that is past. We cannot recall it, but we know that in it we have left undone many duties, and have fallen into many sins, and that all these will rise up against us in judgment. O our Father, we cast the day as a seed into the ground, repenting over all our shortcomings, and trusting humbly in thy mercy, that, while its baser part shall perish, all in it that has been done to thy service shall spring up, and bear fruit an hundred-fold in the future. We thank and adore thee for the mercies with which thou hast this day crowned our lives, and we pray that we may be so filled with thy grace that we may thank and adore thee more and more through all our days on earth. To this end, O God, subdue within us the sinful inclinations of our hearts, and strengthen our unselfish aspirations to thee ; quell our rebellious passion and pride, and quicken our devout affections toward thee and all ·mankind. May the same mind be in us which was in Christ Jesus, — a mind filled with all devout and holy thoughts, with a sweet simplicity, content to do thy manifest will, with a sincerity spotless and pure in all the relations of life, with a spirit of perfect love. Open our spiritual vision, that we may see all men as they appear in thy sight, as the dear children of thy love and the brethren of our Lord and Master Jesus Christ. Help us to resist every inclination of our minds to regard the outward distinctions between man and man. Forgive us when we yield to prejudice or are influenced by pride to despise one of thy little ones. Inspire us with devotedness to thy service here below. Grant us thy aid, that we may not be wanting in any good word and work, which may help to bring thy children nearer to thee.

We commend to thy loving care this night all who are in any sort of need. Comfort those who mourn. Support those who are sorely tried by anxiety, or doubt, or pain of body or of mind. Send thy light to illumine those who are in darkness, and to make the path of duty plain before them.

As we lie down to rest, we ask for thy protection. Refresh our mortal bodies with calm repose; refresh our immortal souls with thy grace and thy peace. Prepare us by our days and nights, by our labor and our repose in this life, for the rest which remaineth for thy people, in the light of thy presence which shineth more and more unto the perfect day.

Hear and accept our prayer, we beseech thee, in the name of Him who is the Life and the Light of men. *Amen.*

LXVIII.

TRUE GAIN.

Sometimes, O Lord, — at least in show, —
A thankful heart we do profess,
When thou such blessings dost bestow
As outward riches, health, or peace ;
But for that means which may conduce
Our souls to their true bliss to raise
We make not very frequent use
Of thankful words or hymns of praise.

Wither.

There is that maketh himself rich, yet hath nothing; there is that maketh himself poor, yet hath great riches.

A little that a righteous man hath is better than the riches of many wicked.

There is that scattereth, and yet increaseth; and there is that withholdeth more than is meet, but it tendeth to poverty.

A good name is rather to be chosen than great riches, and loving favor rather than silver and gold.

Better is a little with righteousness, than great revenues without right.

Lay up for yourself treasures in heaven, where neither moth nor rust doth corrupt, and where thieves do not break through nor steal.

For where your treasure is, there will your heart be also.

If thou hide thy treasure upon the earth, how canst thou expect to find it in heaven? — *Quarles*.

Godliness is great riches, if a man be content with that he hath; for we brought nothing into the world, neither may we carry anything out.

What thou givest to God's glory and thy soul's health is laid up in heaven, that only is thine. — *Quarles*.

Paul desires to know nothing but Christ, and Christ crucified. In this knowledge we possess more than all the sciences and all the riches of the earth can offer us. — *St. Hilary*.

MORNING.

MERCIFUL and Mighty Being! Thou art the perfect and the eternal One! Thou art the Lord and Giver of life! Thou art our Father in heaven! We own, with thankful hearts, thy providential care, and we would begin this day by a renewed consecration of all we are, and of all we have, to thy delightful and reasonable service. O may the Sun of Righteousness arise upon us with healing in his beams! May we see the light of thy truth, and feel the warmth of thy love! Quicken within us all holy desires, strengthen within us all virtuous purposes. Forgive the sins that are past; and help us to profit by our own mistakes, and to be instructed by our own follies. Thou knowest how frail we are, and how short is our time on earth. O teach us so to number our days that we may apply our hearts to the lessons of heavenly wisdom. May we do with our might what our hands find to do, redeeming the passing hours by cheerful diligence, and services of love to thee and to our fellow-men. May we not set our hearts too strongly on the things that perish; may we not be too much lifted up by prosperity, nor too much cast down by adversity, knowing that the fashion of this world passeth away. O Lord, the issues of life and death are thine. Grant us a calm and steady faith in immortality; and may we know ourselves partakers of thy life eternal, through the knowledge of thee and of Jesus Christ, whom thou hast sent. And when we are called away to the unseen world, O may we find ourselves reunited in the larger family of heaven, to share thy glory forevermore. *Amen.*

EVENING.

HOLY Father, whose all-seeing eye has this day marked our words and deeds, and read our secret purposes and desires, forgive us, we pray thee, all that thou hast seen in us this day of evil. And now, before the account of the day is closed, help us, O Father, as we endeavor to judge ourselves, help us to repent of every sin; and should we this night sleep the sleep that knows no earthly awakening, may we die at peace with God, and in charity with all our neighbors. But if thou hast still in store for us days upon earth, help us henceforth to avoid the sins of the past, and daily to grow in the knowledge of thy law, and in likeness to thy holy Son. Blessed be thy name, that thou hast, through him, clearly manifested thyself, and announced to us the great laws of our life, that we should love thee, the Giver of every good gift, and that we should love our neighbors as ourselves. O Holy Father, write these laws upon our hearts. Create us anew, through Christ Jesus, in thine image. Help us to seek with all our hearts thy kingdom, assured that all needful things will be added thereto. Thou art love, fill us with that deep sense of thy mercy which shall awaken our love to thee. Fill us with that love of God that shall lead us to keep thy commandments, with that love of God which leads us to love all thy children. And fill us with that love of thy children which shall show itself in forgetfulness of ourselves, and in unselfish devotion to others' service. O Father, fill us with that perfect love which filled our Lord's heart, and led him to labor and to suffer and to die in behalf of men, and may we honor him by walking in his steps, going about doing good, serving those whom he deigned to call his brethren. And may the blessing which he invoked upon all who believed on him through his Apostle's word descend upon us, and at length upon all mankind, and the world be thus filled with thy glory. *Amen.*

SPECIAL SERVICES.

SPECIAL SERVICES.

I.

SUNDAY MORNING.

Now the shades of night are gone ;
Now the morning light is come ;
Lord, may we be thine to-day,
Drive the shades of sin away.

Fill our souls with heavenly light,
Banish doubt, and clear our sight ;
In thy service, Lord, to-day,
May we stand and watch and pray.

EPISCOPAL COLL.

THOU, Lord, gavest thy people judgment, and true laws, good statutes and commandments : and madest known unto them thy holy Sabbath, and commandedst them precepts, statutes, and laws, by the hand of Moses thy servant.

Thus saith the Lord, Unto them that keep my Sabbaths,. and choose the things that please me, and take hold of my covenant ;

Even unto them will I give, in mine house and within my walls, a place and a name better than of sons and of daughters : I will give them an everlasting name, that shall not be cut off.

Tho same sun arises on this day, and enlightens it; yet because that Sun of Righteousness arose upon it, and gave a new life unto the world in it, and drew the strength of God's moral precept unto it, therefore justly do we sing, with the Psalmist, This is the day which the Lord hath made. — *Bishop Hall.*

Let us have grace whereby we may serve God acceptably, with reverence and godly fear.

God is a spirit, and they that worship him must worship him in spirit and in truth.

O come, let us sing unto the Lord: let us make a joyful noise to the Rock of our salvation.

Let us come before his presence with thanksgiving, and make a joyful noise unto him with psalms.

For the Lord is a great God, and a great King above all gods.

O come, let us worship and bow down : let us kneel before the Lord our Maker.

For he is our God; and we are the people of his pasture, the sheep of his hand.

To-day, if ye will hear his voice, harden not your hearts.

——◆——

O THOU who in the beginning didst cause the light to shine out of darkness, pour into our hearts, with this morning sunlight, the radiance of that revelation which maketh all things new. Thy mercies are new every morning ; may our faith and hope and charity be renewed to-day. Make us new creatures in Christ. This is life eternal, to know thee, the only true God, and Jesus Christ whom thou hast sent. May we learn this day so to know him, and the power of his resurrection, that we shall rise from the bonds of the flesh and the deadness of custom into the life and liberty of the children of God.

God of peace, enable us to return unto our rest this day by waiting on thee without distraction, in the hearty and harmonious devotion of all our faculties and affections to thy service, which is perfect freedom. Guard us from seeking our Sabbath in indolence, which is not our rest. Quicken us to arise and depart out of the very thought of so worshipping thee acceptably, and in the active life of self-discipline, piety, and mercy to honor and use this day in a manner worthy of the Son of man, and grateful to the Father of men.

May we walk in the light of that life and immortality which thy Gospel has opened to the world. May we live above the world, raised by faith to that mountain of the Lord's house, where memory and hope meet and witness to the soul of possessions and pleasures that know no change of time.

May the Sun of Righteousness rise higher and higher over the world, and stretch his healing wings more and more around the hearts and homes and nations of men. Soon may all the families and all the tribes of the earth make one great family in the kingdom of thy Son. May our beloved land soon become his inheritance, and our people that holy and happy people whose God is the Lord. May thy kingdom come on earth, and hasten thou the day when every house shall be a house of God, and every day a Sabbath, and all the thoughts of every heart shall give glory to Him who sitteth on the throne, and to the Lamb for ever and ever. *Amen.*

II.

SUNDAY MORNING.

Blest day of God! most calm, most bright,
'The first and best of days ;
The laborer's rest, the saint's delight,
The day of prayer and praise.
　　　　　　　　　　CODMAN'S COLL.

Prayer, meditation, reading, hearing, preaching, singing, good conference, are the businesses of this day, which I dare not bestow on any work or pleasure, but heavenly. — *Bishop Hall.*

When ye hear the Word of God, surrender yourselves wholly to it, as if for eternity, with a full purpose of will to retain it in your mind, and to order your life according to it. — *Tauler.*

Let us offer the sacrifice of praise to God continually, that is, the fruit of our lips, giving thanks to his name.

But to do good and communicate forget not, for with such sacrifices God is well pleased.

I am the Lord your God; walk in my statutes and keep my judgments, and do them;

And hallow my Sabbaths, and they shall be a sign between me and you, that ye may know that I am the Lord your God.

It is better to plough on holy days than to do nothing, or to do viciously: but let them be spent in the works of the day, that is, in religion and charity. — *Taylor.*

Deliver us, gracious God, from being weary of thy Sabbaths, which are ordained to preserve in our hearts the knowledge of thee, and of thy Son Jesus Christ. — *Wilson.*

O that we may desire and rejoice in the return of this day, and serve thee faithfully on it; and that we may enjoy an everlasting Sabbath with thy saints for Jesus Christ's sake. — *Wilson.*

Serve the Lord with gladness: come before his presence with singing.

Enter into his gates with thanksgiving and into his courts with praise: be thankful unto him, and bless his name.

For the Lord is good; his mercy is everlasting; and his truth endureth to all generations.

———◆———

ETERNAL Spirit of Truth, with reverential thoughts and grateful emotions we bow before thee and invoke thy favor. Be pleased to accept our thanks for the continuance of thy loving-kindness to us through another week. We joyfully hail the return of the day set apart by thy providence for the rest of the weary, for the culture of heavenly good, for the communion of the soul with its inheritance in the skies. May we rightfully improve the precious opportunities of the time. Assist us, Lord, to turn away from vanity, lust, and care, and fix our attention on truth, virtue, and faith, realities of solid and everlasting import. Send thy blessing this day on all ministers of the Gospel and on their congregations. Let thy gracious presence brood over them to make their meditations holy, their worship fervent, their vows effectual, that the kingdom of Christ may be advanced among men. We breathe this prayer as humble disciples of thy Son. O answer us graciously, and thine shall be all the praise. *Amen.*

III.

SUNDAY MORNING.

Sleep, sleep to-day, tormenting cares,
Of earth and folly born !
Ye shall not dim the light that streams
From this celestial morn.

To-morrow will be time enough
To feel your harsh control ;
Ye shall not violate this day,
The Sabbath of the soul.

MRS. BARBAULD.

Six days shalt thou labor and do all thy work; but the seventh day is the Sabbath of the Lord thy God.

O that we may desire and rejoice in the return of this day, and serve thee faithfully on it; that we may enjoy an everlasting Sabbath with thy Saints. — *Wilson.*

Blessed is the man that keepeth the Sabbath from polluting it, and keepeth his hand from doing any evil.

If thou turn away thy foot from the Sabbath, from doing thy pleasure on my holy day; and call the Sabbath a delight, the holy of the Lord, honorable ;

And shalt honor him, not doing thine own ways, nor finding thine own pleasure, nor speaking thine own words ;

Then shalt thou delight thyself in the Lord, for the mouth of the Lord hath spoken it.

And it shall come to pass, that from one Sabbath to another shall all flesh come to worship before me, saith the Lord.

Give unto the Lord the glory due unto his name ; worship the Lord in the beauty of holiness.

Be of a ready heart and mind, free from worldly cares .and thoughts, diligent to hear, careful to mark, studious to remem‑ ber, and desirous to practise all that is commanded, and 'ive according to it :

Do not hear for any other end but to become better in your life, and to be instructed in every good work, and to increase in the love and service of God. — *Taylor.*

Be not carried about with divers and strange doctrines : for it is a good thing that the heart be established with grace.

———◆———

O GOD, thou high and holy one ! With rever‑ ence and gladness and humble love would we unite in thy worship on this hallowed morning. In the spirit of thanksgiving for all thy past mercies would we say, Hitherto hath the Lord helped us ! In tranquil trust would we pray that thou wilt still be our God and guide. With penitent hearts would we ask the pardon of our sins, and grace to reform our lives. O breathe upon us the Holy Spirit ! Renew within us a clean heart. May we to-day enter into the rest that remains for thy peo‑ ple, and enjoy a foretaste of heaven. May our own house be to us as the house of God ; and may our hearts be in tune to join thy public praises.

Be graciously present in every worshipping as‑ sembly ; and may the Gospel message be proclaimed in purity and power. Pity the careless and the prayerless. O send out thy light and thy truth, and bring thy straying children home to their Father's house. Visit with consoling grace the habitations of sorrow. Teach all mankind to love each other as brethren, and to put away the evils which afflict and desolate the earth. May the truths of Christ be welcomed by all people as glad tidings and laws of life.

Father! may our meditations of thee be sweet. May the repose and the instructions of this day strengthen us for the activities and trials of the week, so that all our days may be holy unto the Lord, and all our duties sacred as divine service, fitting us for the purer worship of the upper temple. And to thee be praise everlasting, for the riches of grace and glory bestowed on us through Jesus Christ. *Amen.*

IV.

SUNDAY EVENING.

Glory to thee, my God, this night,
For all the blessings of the light:
Keep us, O keep us, King of kings,
Under thy own almighty wings!

Forgive us, Lord, through thy dear Son,
The ill that we this day have done,
That with the world, ourselves, and thee,
We, ere we sleep, at peace may be.

BISHOP KEN.

From the rising of the sun unto the going down of the same, the Lord's name is to be praised.

Ye that love the Lord, hate evil: he preserveth the souls of his saints; he delivereth them out of the hand of the wicked.

The eyes of the Lord are in every place beholding the evil and the good.

The sacrifice of the wicked is an abomination to the Lord: but the prayer of the upright is his delight.

Seek ye the Lord while he may be found, call ye upon him while he is near.

Thou shalt fear the Lord thy God, and serve him.

Ye shall diligently keep the commandments of the Lord your God, and his testimonies, and his statutes, which he hath commanded thee.

And it shall be our righteousness, if we observe to do all these commandments before the Lord our God, as he hath commanded us.

Heaven and earth shall pass away, but my words shall not pass away.

Jesus said, Whosoever will come after me, let him deny himself, and take up his cross and follow me.

Whosoever shall be ashamed of me, and of my words, of him shall the Son of man be ashamed, when he cometh in the glory of his Father with the holy angels.

Every one that doeth evil hateth the light, neither cometh to the light, lest his deeds should be reproved.

But he that doeth truth, cometh to the light, that his deeds may be made manifest, that they are wrought in God.

———◆———

WE love thee, O our God; and we desire to love thee more and more. Grant to us that we may love thee as much as we desire, and as much as we ought. O love of God, ever burning and never extinguished, fire in the unconsuming bush, inflame, and preserve by inflaming, our hearts. May the tumult of the senses be silent, the fantasies of earth and air be still, and God alone be near to us now.

O dearest Friend, who hast so loved and saved us, who art so vitalizing and uplifting us, the thought of whom is so sweet and always growing sweeter, come with Christ and dwell in our hearts; then thou wilt keep a watch over our lips, our steps, our deeds, and we shall not need to be anxious either for our souls or our bodies.

We have lived, O Lord of light, through another day of thy light. Jesus, our Master, has led us to-day, and we rest in quiet this evening, sitting at his feet, and hearing his words.

Our souls, made in thine image, now feel thee dwelling in them. It is as a drop of water holding in it the image of the sun. Make it more luminous, that thine image in us may be seen by others.

Give us love, sweetest of all gifts, which teaches and learns, and knows no enemy, — love which praises or blames, but never suspects or injures. Give us in our hearts pure love, born of thy love to us, that we may love others as thou lovest us. Give us love, never idle, never weary of well-doing, which never faints or turns or goes backward. Give us love, which flows out equally to old and young, poor and rich, wise and foolish, free and slave, black and white, sick and well, high and low, infidel and saint, good and bad, to the innocent child, and to the abandoned and corrupted sinner. O most loving Father of Jesus Christ, from whom floweth all love, let our hearts, frozen in sin, cold to thee and cold to others, be warmed by this divine fire. So help and bless us in thy Son. *Amen.*

V.

SUNDAY EVENING.

Fading, still fading, the last beam is shining;
Father in heaven! the day is declining;
Safety and innocence flee with the light,
Temptation and danger walk forth with the night;
From the fall of the shade till the mo' ting bells chime,
Shield us from danger and keep us from crime!
Father! have mercy, through Christ Jesus our Lord!

LONGFELLOW'S COLL.

At evening, being the first day of the week, when the doors were shut, came Jesus, and stood in the midst, and saith unto them, Peace be unto you.

Watch, for ye know not what hour your Lord doth come.

Watch and pray, that ye enter not into temptation: the spirit indeed is willing, but the flesh is weak.

Jesus said, They that are whole need not a physician; but they that are sick.

I came not to call the righteous, but sinners, to repentance.

Blessed are they which do hunger and thirst after righteousness, for they shall be filled.

Whosoever cometh to me, and heareth my sayings and doeth them, I will show you to whom he is like.

He is like a man which built an house, and digged deep, and laid the foundation on a rock;

And when the flood arose, the stream beat vehemently upon that house, and could not shake it: for it was founded upon a rock.

T

He that hath my commandments and keepeth them, he it is that loveth me: and he that loveth me shall be loved of my Father, and I will love him, and will manifest myself to him.

Ye are my friends, if ye do whatsoever I command you.

These things I command you, that ye love one another.

———◆———

OUR Father, we kneel before thee in these last moments of the first day, to thank thee for the pure, quiet rest of the Sabbath. For this one day, when we can sit down and be still, and know that thou art God, — can set our life afresh by thine everlasting truth, and wash ourselves from the dust and strife of the world, and be clean. We thank thee, that thou hast made the need for this day a part of our nature, and made the needful day a holy day by thy grace.

We adore thee, that thou hast made it a day when thy children can go home from the school of the world, and be fresh and free for worship in the home, the church, or in the outer temple of nature, — for thoughts of thee, and of the dear ones who have gone from us to thy near presence in heaven. O forgive us if we have broken this good Sabbath by any hard thought or word or deed to men, or by any hard bondage to thee. And may the blessing of this day so blend with the repose of this night, as to make us in the new morning more true and strong for all work of the week to come than we have ever been in the weeks that have gone. This in the spirit of Jesus Christ, thy Son, our Brother. *Amen.*

VI.

SUNDAY EVENING.

Is there a time when moments flow
More lovelily than all beside?
It is, of all the times below,
A Sabbath eve in summer tide.

This day is the scripture fulfilled in your ears.

Thou shalt love the Lord thy God with all thine heart, and with all thy soul, and with all thy might.

And these words which I command thee this day shall be in thine heart:

And thou shalt teach them diligently unto thy children, and shalt talk of them when thou sittest in thine house.

I will call upon God: evening and morning will I pray, and cry aloud: and he shall hear my voice.

Let my prayer be set forth before thee as incense, and the lifting up of my hands as the evening sacrifice.

Whosoever shall not receive the kingdom of God as a little child, he shall not enter therein.

Have faith in God.

For there is one God, and there is none other but he:

And to love him with all the heart, and with all the understanding, and with all the soul, and with all the strength, and to love his neighbor as himself, is more than all whole burnt-offerings and sacrifices.

Blessed are they that hear the Word of God, and keep it.

Jesus spake, saying, I am the light of the world : he that followeth me shall not walk in darkness, but shall have the light of life.

If any man serve me, let him follow me ; and where I am, there shall also my servant be : for if any man serve me, him will my Father honor.

——◆——

O LORD our God, to whom the darkness and the light are both alike, hearken, we humbly beseech thee, to our evening prayer, as with lowly confidence we bow before thee in our domestic sanctuary. We give thee thanks, O God, for the blessed day, consecrated to religious meditation and Christian worship, whose shadows are now gathered around us. We thank thee for all the means of grace and aids to holiness which it brought unto us ; and we pray that thy spirit may seal our hearts with the sanctifying influences of its impressive associations and holy rites, and cause the precious fruits thereof to appear in our lives. If we have heard thy word this day with the outward ear, grant, O Lord, that it may take effect inwardly in our hearts, purging them of all unrighteousness, confirming them in the right faith, quickening them with heavenly hopes, and filling them with comfort, peace, and gladness. But if we have failed to improve our opportunities, and have turned a deaf ear to the voice of Christian instruction, if we have neglected thy word and ordinances, if we have worshipped and served the creature more than the Creator, if we have consulted our ease and pleasure more than our spiritual health and edification, O God, remember not this sin against us, and take not thy Holy Spirit from us; but mercifully forgive us and renew us again unto repentance, that hereafter, remembering the day which thou hast made, we may worthily use it according to thy gracious purpose.

Bless, O God, each member of this household, and so enlighten us with thy wisdom, and imbue us with the Spirit of Christ our Lord, that the outgoing of each morning and the incoming of each evening may find us nearer to the gates of the New Jerusalem, and in closer fellowship with those who have passed from death unto life, and put on the robes of immortality. Shield us from all harm during the night-watches. Fold all who are dear to us in the arms of thy protecting care, and preserve their souls unto eternal life, through thine infinite mercy in Jesus Christ our Lord. *Amen.*

VII.

CHRISTMAS EVE.

Bright was the guiding star that led,
With mild, benignant ray,
The Gentiles to the lowly shed
Where the Redeemer lay.

But lo! a brighter, clearer light
Now points to his abode:
It shines through sin and sorrow's night,
To guide us to our Lord.

SPIRIT OF THE PSALMS.

When Jesus was born in Bethlehem of Judæa, in the days of Herod the king, behold there came wise men from the east to Jerusalem,

Saying, Where is he that is born King of the Jews? for we have seen his star in the east.

And lo, the star which they saw in the east went before them, till it came and stood over where the young child was.

And there were in the same country shepherds abiding in the field, keeping watch over their flock by night.

And lo, the angel of the Lord came upon them, and the glory of the Lord shone round about them; and they were sore afraid.

And the angel said unto them, Fear not: for behold, I bring you good tidings of great joy, which shall be to all people.

For unto you is born this day, in the city of David, a Saviour, which is Christ the Lord.

In this was manifested the love of God towards us, because that God sent his only begotten Son into the world, that we might live through him.

Herein is love, not that we loved God, but that he loved us.

Beloved, if God so loved us, we ought also to love one another.

Blessed be God, even the Father of our Lord Jesus Christ, the Father of mercies, and the God of all comfort.

Ye know the grace of our Lord Jesus Christ, that though he was rich, yet for your sakes he became poor, that ye through his poverty might be rich.

———◆———

ALMIGHTY God, our Father in heaven, Creator of all worlds, thou dost make manifest thy power and wisdom and goodness most abundantly in the bestowal of life, and above all in the life of thy rational creatures, not only creatures of thine, but children. We bless thee for all thy mercies to us and our race through birth. We rejoice that, much as we are commanded to labor and make the best use of our talents, thou dost enrich us from the very beginning in the endowments of our own nature, and the treasures of genius and grace that are born into the world from the fulness of thy light and love. This night, as we meditate upon the nativity of thy beloved Son, we bless thee for all thy chosen servants, patriarchs, law-givers, prophets, sages, bards, godly and gifted men and women, who, by birth as well as nature, were sent to prepare his way or speed his work.

We give thee thanks for the mighty yearning of the human heart for the coming of a Saviour, and the constant promise of thy word that he was to come. In our own souls this night we repeat the humble sighs and panting aspirations of ancient men and ages, and own that our souls are in darkness and infirmity, without faith in Him who comes to bring God to man and man to God. We bless thee for the tribute that we can pay to him from our very sense of need and dependence, and that our own hearts can so answer from their wilderness the precursor's cry, " Prepare ye the way of the Lord." In us the rough places are to be made smooth, the crooked straight, the mountains of pride brought low, and the valleys of despondency lifted up. O God, prepare thou the way in us now, and may we welcome anew thy Holy Child. Hosanna! blessed be he who cometh in the name of the Lord!

We give thee thanks this night for our home-blessings, and especially for all birth-gifts to us and our children, through native talents and dispositions. We bless thee that thou hast still more largely endowed us than by our own nature, by making us heirs, — joint-heirs in the riches born into the world in Jesus Christ. We rejoice that in him we may be made whole, and that not only by his godly example and spotless life and sacrificial death, but also by his nativity, we are enriched and comforted. We ask for thy grace to help us understand and enjoy more deeply and truly the day of his birth, and to praise thee, not only for what he did for us by his work, but what thou didst for him and for us in his very being. O God, our Father in heaven, quicken within us the childlike spirit, that by more filial trust in thee we may enter into the life of thy beloved Son, and learn how precious to us is that Divine Sonship that rebukes and corrects the frailties of our nature, and presents us in our accepted Head before thee as the children of heavenly adoption.

We offer this, our prayer, in the name of thy holy child Jesus, and trusting in the fellowship of thy Holy Spirit. *Amen.*

VIII.

CHRISTMAS MORNING.

Hail! hail, auspicious morn!
The Saviour Christ is born!
(Such was the immortal seraph's song sublime ;)
Glory to God in heaven !
On earth sweet peace be given,
Sweet peace and friendship to the end of time !

DR. GARDINER, *from Milton.*

How beautiful upon the mountains are the feet of him that bringeth good tidings, that publisheth peace ; that publisheth salvation ; that saith unto Zion, Thy God reigneth.

The Lord hath comforted his people.

For God so loved the world, that he gave his only begotten Son, that whosoever believeth in him should not perish, but have everlasting life.

All the ends of the earth shall see the salvation of our God.

Glory to God in the highest, and on earth peace, good-will to men.

For God, who commanded the light to shine out of darkness, hath shined in our hearts, to give the light of the knowledge of the glory of God in the face of Jesus Christ.

Thanks be to God for his unspeakable gift.

This is a faithful saying, and worthy of all acceptation, that Christ Jesus came into the world to save sinners.

Let the word of Christ dwell in you richly in all wisdom ; teaching and admonishing one another in psalms and hymns, and spiritual songs, singing with grace in your hearts to the Lord.

And whatsoever ye do in word or deed, do all in the name of the Lord Jesus, giving thanks to God and the Father by him.

Whosoever would fully and feelingly understand the words of Christ, must endeavor to conform his life wholly to the life of Christ. — *À Kempis.*

As ye have therefore received Christ Jesus the Lord, so walk ye in him :

Rooted and built up in him, and stablished in the faith, as ye have been taught, abounding therein, with thanksgiving.

I can do all things through Christ, which strengtheneth me.

——◆——

O THOU, who art the Source of all life! with the coming of this morning we humbly acknowledge the chiefest expression of thy paternal tenderness. We bless thee for the incarnation of thy ceaseless love in Jesus Christ. We bless thee for his advent as the manifestation of thyself, thine unforgetful care and merciful purposes. In our darkness, thou hast sent us the light. In our ignorance, thou hast given us the truth. In our fears, thou hast cheered us with the hope of immortality. For the birth of the Teacher of thy wisdom, for Him who has shown us the Father, we bring thee the sacrifice of thanksgiving. We rejoice in the Day-spring from on high. For the doings of the

Word made flesh our praises ascend to thee, the Infinite Fountain of all blessedness! We offer unto thee the tribute of gratitude for the glad tidings and for all their benignant influences. We recognize thy near and gracious providence in the introduction and spread of the Gospel, and in all that it has done for mankind! To thee we owe the humane and fraternal spirit it has inculcated and cherished; its promises of forgiveness to the penitent; its consolations for the afflicted; its rest for the weary and heavy-laden; its promises of the better life to come! Especially, O Thou who hast set the solitary in families, would we this day remember our indebtedness to thee, for the kindly sympathies, the mutual helpfulness, the sweet privileges, the near and endearing relations, which enrich the Christian home. For the Man of Sorrows, who was acquainted with grief and touched with a feeling of our infirmities; for Him who took little children in his arms, and assured us that of such is the kingdom of heaven; for the Friend who hath said, " Thy brother shall rise again "; for Him who has thus sanctified and encouraged our purest affections, and lifted them above the conceptions of earth and the fear of the grave, — we render unto thee the praise of trustful hearts. Increase, we beseech thee, our faith in Jesus; help us to be his obedient disciples, that we may be admitted to the mansions of his Father's house. And grant, O

God, that the purposes of the Saviour's mission may be fulfilled, till everywhere there shall be Glory to thee in the highest, peace on earth, and good-will toward men. *Amen.*

IX.

NEW YEAR'S EVE.

O God ! to thee our hearts would pay
Their gratitude sincere,
Whose love hath kept us, night and day,
Throughout another year.

For joy and grief alike we pay
Our thanks to thee above ;
And only pray to grow each day
More worthy of thy love.
GASKELL.

It is of the Lord's mercies that we are not consumed, because his compassions fail not.

They are new every morning.

Thou crownest the year with thy goodness.

The Lord is good unto them that wait for him, to the soul that seeketh him.

Let us lift up our heart with our hands unto God in the heavens.

Behold God is great; we know him not, neither can the number of his years be searched out.

When a few years are come, then I shall go the way whence I shall not return.

The days of our years are threescore years and ten; and if by reason of strength they be fourscore years, yet is their strength labor and sorrow; for it is soon cut off, and we fly away.

So teach us to number our days, that we may apply our hearts unto wisdom.

O satisfy our souls with thy mercy, that we may rejoice and be glad all our days.

We are strangers and sojourners, as were all our fathers; our days on the earth are as a shadow, and there is none abiding.

Who knoweth what is good for man in this life, all the days of his vain life which he spendeth as a shadow.

This very instability of human things, O God, is in the perfections of thy decrees, that by it we may be compelled to seek after solid and unchangeable good. — *St. Gregory.*

Thou art my hope, O Lord God, thou art my trust.

Blessed be the Lord, for he hath showed me his marvellous kindness.

——◆——

O EVER–KIND, ever-loving, but ever-holy God, how can we render unto thee fit thanks for thine unmeasured mercy, how acknowledge with due humility our unworthiness and sin! At every station upon our journey of life, as we pause and look over the past, we see the crowded tokens of thy loving-kindness, thy tender care, thy watchful providence, and we recall also abundant memories

of our errors, our short-comings, and our transgressions. We would, O Father, return thee thanks
for all that we have hitherto enjoyed, and for every
opportunity which thou hast granted us for becoming or for doing good. For the supply of our daily
needs, and for all that thou hast added of the comforts and joys of life, for all that has charmed the
eye and the ear, for the treasures of knowledge and
wisdom, for the affections that bind us together, and
for the hope given through our Lord Jesus, that
those who love him and love each other shall have
eternal communion and fellowship with each other
and with him; for these, and for every other gift of
thy providence and of thy grace, we would give
thee thanks, and we pray thee that thy good spirit
may help us show our gratitude by obedience to thy
commands.

Holy Father, forgive us the sins of the past, and
if thou dost allow us to see, still longer, days upon
earth, help us to spend them in thy service. May
the year that is coming find us watchful to learn
what is thy will, and to keep thy commandments.
Help us to be helpers of each other in all that is
good, and to be helpers of all men as we have
opportunity; and if thou shouldst spare us to see
many years upon earth, may each one find us more
watchful over ourselves, more resigned to thy will,
more zealous in thy service, more observant of
opportunities to do good. *Amen.*

X.

NEW YEAR'S DAY.

Spared to see another year,
Let thy blessing meet us here ;
Come, thy dying work revive,
Bid thy drooping garden thrive ;
Sun of righteousness, arise !
Warm our hearts, and bless our eyes ;
Let our prayer thy mercy move,
Make this year a time of love.

OLNEY'S HYMNS.

Jesus spake also this parable : A certain man had a fig-tree planted in his vineyard; and he came and sought fruit thereon and found none.

Then said he unto the dresser of his vineyard, Behold, these three years I came seeking fruit on this fig-tree, and find none; cut it down; why cumbereth it the ground.

And he, answering, said unto him, Lord, let it alone this year also, till I shall dig about it and dung it.

And if it bear fruit, well; and if not, then after that thou shalt cut it down.

O my God, take me not away in the midst of my days; thy years are throughout all generations.

The Lord is very pitiful, and of tender mercy.

If every year we would root out one vice, we should sooner become perfect men. — *À Kempis.*

Alas ! length of days doth more often make our sins the greater than our lives the better. — *À Kempis.*

O send out thy light and thy truth; let them lead me; let them bring me unto thy holy hill, and to thy tabernacles.

Awake thou that sleepest, and arise from the dead, and Christ shall give thee light.

See, then, that ye walk circumspectly, not as fools, but as wise, redeeming the time; and if ye call on the Father, who without respect of persons judgeth according to every man's work, pass the time of your sojourning here in fear.

For the time past of our life may suffice us to have wrought the will of the Gentiles.

Wherefore, laying aside all malice, and all guile, and all envies, and all evil speakings;

Having your conversation honest, honor all men, love the brotherhood, fear God.

MORNING.

O THOU who art our Dwelling-place in all generations, we rejoice in the light of this new day, and with grateful and devout minds we would acknowledge thy love in all the vicissitudes of our earthly lot, whether it be in the changing year, the procession of the seasons, summer and winter, day and night, or in our lives as we feel the motion of thy providence in time and events. O God, we thank thee, we bless thee, for that gentle influence and happy inclination of human life, by which our increasing days bring into our souls a deeper sense of the great spiritual realities, by which the glaring light of this world becomes softened, and the powers of the world to come are manifest in the upper deep. In harmony with this spirit and temper of our life, as directed by thee, we would stand in reverence, gratitude, and joy upon the borders of a new year : with reverence, because of thy power mingled in the stream of our lives ; with gratitude, because of thy love ; with joy, because of our building of God, our house not made with hands. O God, as we feel the insecurity of all things below, may the bright foundations of the eternal city be firm and glorious. May we not repine at the swiftness of our mortal days, but live the life of the spirit in the eternal now of God. Whatever new experiences the past year has brought, may they descend in wisdom and blessing on teachable and childlike hearts. Help us to call to mind our errors, our follies, and our sins, and in penitence to seek thy forgiveness.

We ask thy blessing upon us in the mutual congratulations and joys of the season. May they not be formal, but the warm and honest gush of good hearts, that love God and wish all his children well. O be patient with the thoughtless, and give them such experience as shall bring into their souls a subdued and steady strength. We would begin the year with new trust in thee ; and help us, O God, to bring our lives up to our thought. *Amen.*

EVENING.

ETERNAL God! thou who art the same yesterday, to-day, and forever, and with whom is no variableness nor shadow of turning, to thee be glory and honor, dominion and power everlasting. We have entered upon the life of the new year, and tried the experiment of our new resolutions for the day that is now closing. Heavenly Father, has it been more acceptable in thy sight than the days of the year that is now past forever? Have we more earnestly worked, or more fondly prayed, or more glorified thy name through this day's life, than in that former time over which we now mourn? Help us to hear the answer of thy Holy Spirit, as it whispers to our souls its approbation or rebuke. For, O our Father, we would not live without growing better and wiser and purer, through the discipline of our daily life, or without feeling, as time passes and days and years are numbered, that we are finding a harmonious residence in thy kingdom of Nature and Providence. We would learn to live more and more in the things which do not perish with the using, things which change not with time; not in things which are seen, for they are temporal, but in things which are not seen, for they are eternal. To this end, bless our evening worship; to this end sanctify all our experiences of joy or sorrow, that, while all things else grow old and die with the changing years, our lives may be calm, strong, and peaceful, because hid with Christ in God. May we find comfort and help in the tranquillity and immensity of thy creation, and feel ourselves a part of a beneficent order, wherein not an atom nor a star can perish. But O enable us to find a still higher consolation in the sweet thought that thou art with us, not only as thou art with the atom and the star, but as a father and friend, guiding and saving us. May we lie down to sleep this night, feeling that all our sins have been forgiven, and that we may try the experiment of life anew on the morrow. Bless all who are dear to us; and, when life's anxious scene is over, take us to thyself, and to thee shall be the glory forever. *Amen.*

XI.

THANKSGIVING–DAY MORNING.

All that spring with bounteous hand
Scatters o'er the smiling land ;
All that liberal autumn pours
From her rich o'erflowing stores ;

These to thee, our God ! we owe,
Source whence all our blessings flow !
And for these our souls shall raise
Grateful vows and solemn praise.

MRS. BARBAULD.

The Lord said in his heart, While the earth remaineth, seed-time and harvest, and cold and heat, and summer and winter, and day and night shall not cease.

Let us now fear the Lord our God, that giveth rain, both the former and the latter, in his season; he reserveth unto us the appointed weeks of his harvest.

Be thou exalted, O God, above the heavens; let thy glory be above all the earth.

What thanks can we render to God ?

Let us offer the sacrifice of praise to God continually, that is, the fruit of our lips, giving thanks to his name.

In psalms, and hymns, and spiritual songs, singing and making melody in your heart to the Lord.

Giving thanks always for all things unto God and the Father, in the name of our Lord Jesus.

Honor the Lord with thy substance, and with the first-fruits of all thine increase.

So shall thy barns be filled with plenty.

And ye shall eat in plenty, and be satisfied, and praise the name of the Lord your God, that hath dealt wondrously with you.

O merciful Father, give me grace for the time to come to observe and to value thy kindnesses, as becomes one who has received so much more than he deserves. — *Wilson.*

——◆——

ALMIGHTY and most merciful God: thou who art the Fountain of all blessedness and the Giver of every good and every perfect gift, with grateful hearts we come before thee to acknowledge thy goodness and to ascribe praise to thy great and holy name. We thank thee that thou hast permitted us to behold the light of another morning. We thank thee for another return of this day in which we are to commemorate the tokens of thy love to us, and for all its sacred interests and associations.

How precious have been thy thoughts unto us, O God, how great has been the sum of them. We praise thee, we bless thee, that thou hast given us peace within our borders, and health in our habitation; that thou hast preserved to us the privileges of civil and religious liberty; that thou hast fulfilled thy promise of old, that, while the earth remaineth, seed-time and harvest shall never cease; that thou hast afforded us so many opportunities for usefulness, for improvement, and for happiness. How constant has been thy care, how ceaseless thy providence, how unremitting thy love. We would call upon our souls and all that is within us to praise thee and to bless thy name forevermore.

Impress upon our minds more deeply, we beseech thee, O God, our dependence upon thee. Enable us to realize more fully that it is in thee we live and move and have our being; that we are indebted to thee for all our privileges and all our enjoyments; for the sacred interests of home; for the pleasures of social intercourse; for opportunities for doing good; for the means of grace and the hope of glory.

Wilt thou continue thy favors to us, O Father? and lead us into the paths of righteousness, truth, and peace.

We would remember before thee our friends, and all who are near and dear to us; and whatsoever things we ask for ourselves, we beseech thee to grant unto them.

And may thy kingdom come, and thy will be done here on earth as it is done in heaven. And unto thee, through Jesus Christ our Saviour, shall be given all praise evermore. *Amen.*

XII.

THANKSGIVING–DAY EVENING.

Great Source of unexhausted good,
Who giv'st us health and friends and food,
   And peace, and calm content,
Like fragrant incense, to the skies,
Let songs of grateful praises rise
   For all thy blessings lent.

EXETER COLL.

Blessed is the man that trusteth in the Lord, and whoso hope the Lord is.

For he shall be as a tree planted by the waters.

Two things have I required of thee; deny me them not.

Remove me far from vanity and lies; give me neither poverty nor riches; feed me with food convenient for me.

Lest I be full and deny thee, and say, Who is the Lord? or lest I be poor and steal, and take the name of the Lord in vain.

Keep me under the protection of thy good providence, and make me to have a perpetual fear and love of thy holy name. — *Wilson.*

Give me grace never to condemn thy providence; let me adore the wisdom of thy conduct, the holiness of thy ways, and the power of thy grace. — *Wilson.*

Trust in the Lord and do good; so shalt thou dwell in the Lord, and verily thou shalt be fed.

Consider the ravens; for they neither sow nor reap; which

neither have storehouse nor barn; and God feedeth them; how much more are ye better than the fowls.

Seek not ye what ye shall eat, or what ye shall drink, neither be ye of doubtful mind.

But rather seek ye the kingdom of God, and all these things shall be added unto you.

Praise the Lord, call upon his name, declare his doings among the people.

Sing unto the Lord; for he hath done excellent things; this is known in all the earth.

———◆———

WE thank thee, our Heavenly Father, for the enjoyments of this day. May our hearts rejoice in the Lord, and our souls be glad in the God of their salvation. Thou hast crowned the year with thy goodness, and under thy watchful providence our paths are enriched with all things needful. Thou hast spread our table with thy bounties, and made our cups to run over. We desire to add to our happiness a holier joy, by acknowledging thee to be the Author of it and of all good. May our use of thy gifts not end in sensual enjoyment, may they be regarded as motives to gratitude, and as tokens of the love which blesses us always. May it be our prayer and earnest desire that thy kingdom may come in our hearts and our home, that kingdom which is not meat or drink, but righteousness and peace and joy in the Holy Spirit.

And we pray that thy goodness, in the providence that every day sustains us, and blesses us in ways so manifold, may nourish in us a grateful and affectionate spirit, may lead us to repentance for our sins, and to a deep and living faith in thee.

Thou hast permitted us to see each others' faces to-day in peace and happiness, and to spend the hours in glad and loving intercourse. May our love be quickened and our affections made purer by the happy memories of the day. May the joy we have felt abide in us, drawing us nearer in love and mutual kindness in the days to come, so that we shall be preparing, as time passes, for the perfect communion, the unbroken friendship, and ceaseless thanksgiving of heaven.

We remember with tenderness and affection those with us in former years, but now gone from our earthly acquaintance. They are not lost, we do not mourn for them. We pray that thou wilt keep our love unwasted and unchanged till we meet them again in a better world. May we so live now that our souls may be in fellowship with their glorified spirits.

O our Father, whose loving-kindness has given that for which we have so much reason to be thankful, let not our gratitude end with this day. May this be the emblem of each day to come, and may the spirit of this happy festival brighten and cheer our home as each new day reveals new proofs of thy love.

Take us into thy holy keeping this night, may thine angels defend us. Let thy peace descend into our hearts, as sleep falls on our eyelids. We rest in thee, and thine everlasting arms are our refuge. Keep us in life or take us in death, that, living or dying, we may be ever with thee.

In the name of Jesus Christ, through whom we know thee, our Father, we offer our prayer, and ascribe to thee and to him honor and glory and power now and evermore. *Amen.*

XIII.

FAST-DAY.

Is this a fast, to keep
The larder lean,
And clean
From fat of neats and sheep?

Is it to fast an hour,
Or ragged to go,
Or show
A downcast look and sour?

It is to fast from strife,
From old debate
And hate;
To circumcise thy life;

> *To starve thy sin,*
> *Not bin:*
> *And that's to keep thy Lent!*
>
> HERRICK.

Sanctify ye a fast, call a solemn assembly, gather the elders and all the inhabitants of the land unto the house of the Lord your God, and cry unto the Lord.

Now, saith the Lord, Turn ye even to me with all your heart, and with fasting, and with weeping, and with mourning;

And rend your hearts and not your garments, and turn unto the Lord your God; for he is gracious and merciful, slow to anger, and of great kindness.

Is not this the fast that I have chosen? to loose the bands of wickedness, to undo the heavy burdens, and to let the oppressed go free?

Is it not to deal thy bread to the hungry, and that thou bring the poor that are cast out to thy house?

To do justice and judgment is more acceptable to the Lord than sacrifice.

Thus saith the Lord of Hosts, Turn ye now from your evil ways, and from your evil doings.

Turn ye unto me, saith the Lord of hosts, and I will turn unto you.

These are the things that ye shall do; speak ye every man the truth to his neighbor; execute the judgment of truth and peace in your gates;

And let none imagine evil in your hearts, for these things I hate, saith the Lord.

And the work of righteousness shall be peace; and the effect of righteousness, quietness and assurance forever.

And my people shall dwell in a peaceable habitation, and in sure dwellings, and in quiet resting-places.

MORNING.

IN a spirit of humility and contrition, we come into thy presence, O Lord, our Heavenly Father. We feel our dependence upon thee for all that we are and all that we have. We acknowledge our unworthiness, our weakness, and our sin. We are humiliated in our sense of defeat in many a struggle and conflict. Yet we know that thou art long-suffering with us, and full of compassion. Thine infinite pity reaches down to our low estate, and thou dost raise us from our despondency and doubt and sin. Like as a father pitieth his children, so dost thou pity us, thy children. As far as the east is from the west, so far dost thou remove our transgressions from us. May we feel thy pardoning mercy softening our hearts to penitence, and assuring us of a gracious forgiveness.

We remember before thee the condition and needs of our beloved country. We feel, that, as a people, we have sinned in thy sight. We have forgotten thy holy laws. We have neglected thy commandments. In our love of the world, in our service of mammon, in our lust for power, we have forsaken thy statutes. We have followed the devices of our own hearts, and have sinned against thy perfect will. Deliver us, O Father from the fruit of our doings. Grant that our sins may not be laid up against us. Help us by a timely repentance, which shall be full of good works, to turn aside the consequences of our wrong-doings. Bring in upon us the blessings of an impartial freedom, and the righteousness of the kingdom of God. Make us faithful to the great duties before us, that in the generations to come the land will be filled with thy glory and the happiness of all our brethren. May slavery and oppression come to an end throughout our borders. Hush all contention and strife, and fill the hearts of all our people with that peace which passeth understanding, and which shall keep us from all evil evermore.

Graciously remember thy servant, the President of the United States, and all who are joined with him in counsel and authority. Be a safeguard and a shield to our armies and to those that are afar off upon the sea. Guide with wisdom the Governor of our Commonwealth and his associates in the service of the State. Be with all kings and princes, and all peoples and tribes and nations on the face of the whole earth, and fill the world with the glory and goodness of thy holy name.

May our penitence, our piety, and our prayerfulness, our fidelity, our firmness in all things good, and our faith in thee, work out for us a complete salvation from every sin, and an abundant entrance into thy kingdom above. We offer our petitions and ask thy blessing and thy help forevermore, through Jesus Christ our Lord. *Amen.*

EVENING.

O THOU who art our God, as thou hast been the God of our fathers, we would bow ourselves before thee with penitent and contrite hearts. We acknowledge our transgressions. We have sinned against heaven and in thy sight. We deserve thy chastisements. Look down upon us, we beseech thee, not in judgment, but in mercy. Remember not the sins of our youth nor our transgressions; save us from our sins, and blot out all our iniquities. According to thy mercy, remember thou us for thy goodness' sake, O Lord.

Look in kindness on our country. As a people we thank thee for all that thou hast been to us and our fathers. We praise and bless thee for the gifts of thy love and the privileges which thou hast bestowed upon us, — for this goodly land, for the abundance with which thou hast crowned our labors, for our government, with its benign and protecting care over us, for the blessings of civil and religious liberty, for our social advantages, for our schools and churches, for the Christian homes in which we have been nurtured, for the means of grace, and the hope of glory.

While we thank thee for these thy gifts and mercies, we confess, with humiliation and sorrow, that we have not improved as we ought the opportunities and privileges which thou hast bestowed, that we have been less careful to impart thy gifts to others than to appropriate them to ourselves, and that we have not accepted and taken home to our hearts, as we ought, thine offers of grace and pardon and eternal life in Jesus Christ. Forgive us, we entreat thee, all this our unworthiness. May we truly repent of our sins. And grant that, in all time to come, we may be more faithful and true to thee, that we may love thee with a more earnest love, and give ourselves to thee in our daily life with a more hearty and entire devotion. Turn from us, O God, those judgments which we most truly have deserved. Save our country from the dangers impending over it. Grant that our rulers and lawgivers and judges may be wise and just. May we extend to all within our borders the advantages of liberty and law which we ask for ourselves, and so live as a people, that we may be a joy and a blessing among the families of the earth, that thy peace may be within our walls, thy prosperity within our palaces, and that the blessing of those who are ready to perish may go with us, through the riches of thy love in Jesus Christ our Lord. *Amen.*

THE END.